FLIP OR HOLD
THE ROAD TO GOLD

A TREASURE MAP TO
REAL ESTATE INVESTMENT RICHES FOR NEW INVESTORS

WHAT OTHERS HAVE SAID ABOUT FRED TICHAUER

Fred is very professional, attentive to detail, and very easy to work with. Fred is a straight shooter and extremely honest. The process was incredibly easy, and he was very responsive and thorough. I can recommend him to anyone seeking a professional Realtor.

Mike Bierman
MJCH LLC

The author, Fred Tichauer, has been instrumental in locating and negotiating contracts for houses which I have purchased for 38 years. His depth of real estate knowledge is exceptional; he is an expert in both residential and investment properties. His assessment of property value is factual and deliberate. Fred shares his knowledge, insight, and experience in this book. Reading it will serve you well in the real estate field.

Dr. Joe L. Davis
Professor Emeritus, University of Nebraska–Omaha

After retiring from the National Football League, I wanted to find a way to make money without being stuck behind a desk. I was always interested in real estate but had no experience prior to being introduced to Fred Tichauer. Not only did Fred walk me through every step of buying and holding real estate, but we built a genuine friendship along the way. He does not just talk a big game, he lives it, being an investor himself. I never thought I would be able to expand my financial portfolio to this extent so quickly. Having the best mentor along with hard work, and here I stand corrected. Fred Tichauer, second to none!

Kenny Onatolu
Retired Linebacker, National Football League

I always wanted to own real estate but did not know how to get started. I met Fred Tichauer 13 years ago. Fred listened to my needs and wants, and he helped me understand that the best investment opportunities were with single-family homes. He taught me how to buy foreclosed properties with little to no money down, and he provided me with the resources and ongoing support to be successful. The first couple of properties were a learning experience, but once I figured out the system, I was able to rapidly grow my portfolio. I had many growth spurts where I doubled my portfolio size, and Fred supported me and provided guidance along the way. Today, I own 23 single-family homes with equity over 1 million dollars. There is no way I would ever be able to create a business with that kind of value with a limited investment. Fred taught me how to leverage my strong financial situation and use that to purchase real estate. Fred is also one of my closest friends, so not only did he help me become a millionaire, but I have a great friend for life. Thanks, Fred, for being my mentor!

Scott Simon
Simon Holdings LLC

As we were purchasing rental properties through our Self-Directed 401k, finding someone like Fred was key to our success. Fred understood the intricacies of using 401k monies to purchase rentals as an investment and how it was different from purchasing properties with post-tax monies. Fred went above and beyond in supporting and guiding us through two trips to Omaha and multiple home purchases and securing an excellent property manager. Even after the purchases were made, he continues to check in with us to see how our investments are going. Working with Fred is the best first step any real estate investor could make!

Vaughn Hollingsworth
Travel Designer / Franchise Owner
Cruise Planners

Fred is one of the most influential people I have ever met in my life. I was lucky to have met Fred five years ago. Since that time, he has guided me step-by-step through many real estate transactions with each one having a different obstacle to overcome. He has showed me how to methodically build a steady stream of passive income through investing in single-family homes. This has provided my family and I true financial freedom. I never thought I could consider retiring before 40, but now it is a very realistic goal. Fred will always be someone I look up to for his strong work ethic, honesty, and true passion for helping people like me achieve their dreams.

Andy Terry
Full-time Investor

We are on our way to financial freedom because of Fred! Fred's knowledge and guidance have been instrumental to starting and developing our future in real estate investing. Over the past year, Fred has guided us through every step of the process of turning run-down houses into beautiful rental homes that create instant cash-flow machines. We have sincerely enjoyed getting to know Fred and working with him, and we are beyond grateful for his professionalism, expertise, and commitment to our success. Every step of the way, he has been there for us and goes above and beyond to provide us with the tools, resources, and support to be successful. We cannot say enough about Fred's extensive knowledge and experience, passion for real estate investing, and dedication to his clients. We consider Fred to be a mentor and friend and are so thankful for all he has done for us on this incredible real estate journey!

Chris and Lavin Haberling

Fred Tichauer has been indispensable in growing our portfolio over the past 10 years. His approach to serving his clients by using an investor's mindset when analyzing opportunities has helped us navigate difficult markets, saving us an untold amount of hours and money.

Jason Bogner
Rolls Properties LLC

Fred's help was invaluable in getting us started with our rental houses. He was quick to steer us away from houses that had problems we would have overlooked, and recommended things we could do to increase the value of the properties we purchased.

Jim and Lynda Madison

I have had the opportunity to work with Fred for nearly 17 years. Over that period, he has been both an asset and an inspiration. To date, I have bought and sold more than 180 homes and acquired a respectable rental portfolio. We may have disagreed from time to time on a project; however, Fred's desire to see those around him succeed has always shone through. His need to share his knowledge of this changing industry is truly selfless. I wish Fred all the success in the world on his crusade to broaden others' knowledge and abilities by sharing his insight and time.

Doug Riddington
K. R. Prop. LLC
DJTL Prop. LLC

It has been an honor to have been introduced to Fred. He had guided me in several real estate decisions and continues to do so. He is very knowledgeable and always willing to offer his advice and help. I highly recommend Fred if you are looking to learn while also buying and selling properties.

Angela Novotny Arkfeld

Our relationship with Fred began with a referral from a banker and developed into a friendship. The first business encounter began at a coffee shop, and we knew from that first meeting that the honesty, knowledge, and transparency Fred shared was genuine. We were in the infancy of creating a reputable rental business and beginning the process of building a long-term team to help develop, strengthen, and materialize our vision. Fred's years in the business and willingness to share his experiences have been priceless in our journey. His down-to-earth business sense has contributed to our success, and we are truly blessed with the continuous support (both professionally and personally).

Scott and Tammy Penix

Fred is absolutely amazing to work with! As a first-time out-of-state buyer I discovered that there were many things I did not know, and Fred and Kelly were incredibly responsive 100% of the way through the purchase process and beyond. If I had been aware that buying in Omaha could be this hassle-free, I would have done so years ago. Fred does an amazing job negotiating on behalf of his clients, and he's so skilled in his knowledge about investment properties that I would gladly attend any class that this man would facilitate. Truly priceless information that I've never experienced when working with other agents. Fred has a deep knowledge about everything under the sun regarding real estate, lenders, construction, inspections, property management, and insurance. Not surprisingly, several lenders that I had contacted when shopping for rates knew of Fred and talked about how outstanding he is. There were countless instances where Fred went above and beyond in looking out for my best interests, and the same could not be said for other agents I've worked with in the past. If every agent ran their business the way Fred does, I think no one would have to market themselves; instead, their entire business would be developed on referrals. A friend referred me to Fred, and they had been referred to him. I also plan to refer several people to him as well. Fred is also very positive, and it's nice to work with someone where you never feel like you're a bother and that you're in a truly great business partnership. I recommend Fred Tichauer for all needs real estate related, and I will be his client again at the drop of a hat!

Maria Sams

Fred has incorporated his years of investment experience into a simple, easy-to-follow process. My husband and I have used his process to develop an investment strategy, partner with a local bank, and purchase our first rental property. Fred's guidance towards purchasing the right home and analyzing the cost to renovate provided us the opportunity to cash flow immediately from our rental property and have over $30,000 in equity when refinancing. His guidance is priceless and full proof when followed properly.

Wendy Ditoro
Realtor, Keller Williams Greater Omaha

I have not come across many people like Fred. His wealth of knowledge about real estate investment is deep and wide. Furthermore, his willingness to share that knowledge is unlike another! This man is of great integrity and knows what he is doing. The best part is that he is willing to lovingly share his experience and knowledge with anyone who is willing to be a student. Fred's desire to help everyone become the best version of themselves and accomplish the American Dream is unmistakable.

Liz Kelly
Realtor since 2003

Fred's enthusiasm and knowledge of investing in single-family properties is unrivaled, and I applaud his willingness to share 40+ years of experience with others through this book and in the classroom. I routinely have Fred speak to our students about the subject... many respond accordingly by acquiring their first investment property before graduation.

David Beberwyk
Real Estate Program Director, University of Nebraska–Omaha

Fred has made many friends, admirers, and followers over his long and productive real estate career. He attracts people because he is very competent, honest, and works hard to help others succeed. Anyone who spends some serious time studying and applying the materials in this book will get to know Fred and like him, too. Plus, there is a rewarding professional life waiting for you to enjoy.

Dean Uhing
Associate Broker, Realtor, Builder, Adjunct Faculty with
Metropolitan Community College in Omaha, Nebraska

I am a licensed real estate broker. My background for over a decade is in the management of commercial property. My real estate license allows me to buy, sell, lease, and manage property, and to help others do the same.

Even though I can buy my own investment property, I choose to work with Fred Tichauer on residential properties. I appreciate the depth of knowledge he has in this area. He helps me locate, purchase, and then sell residential properties. My education in real estate puts me at a point where I see the benefit of working with a professional in the specific area of buying and selling homes. I am looking for the best-fitting deal in the market. I do not just try to do it on my own because my license says I can. Working with Fred and his team gives me a good return on my investment.

John Krecek
Broker, Custom Realty

As a single, self-employed woman I've spent much time worrying about how to feel more secure about my financial future. Being a real estate professional, I know that real estate is a great investment, but I've been unable to move forward because of the paralyzing fear of making the wrong investment decision. Fred Tichauer's books and his classes have given me the tools and the confidence I needed to pull the trigger. I now have two multi-family investment properties and enough equity to purchase a third with no money out of pocket. In two short years I've defined my retirement goals and moved them much closer to a reality instead of an uncertain hope and a prayer.

Julie Lauritsen
Real Estate Agent
Berkshire Hathaway Ambassador Real Estate

Fred truly is the expert in helping colleagues, clients, friends, and family with their wealth planning. His passion for sharing the success that he has had with investment properties with others is such an awesome gift. The knowledge, experience, and expertise that he has in this field is invaluable, and I am very thankful for his mentorship. You won't regret reading this book. It will change your life and the lives of those you love because real estate is a solid investment that you know you can count on when it comes time for you to retire, and Fred has mastered it. He is a one-of-a-kind gem, and both my father, Vaughn Wiebusch, and I are very thankful for him.

Anna Lemieux
Team Wiebusch
Re/Max Results

"I wish I had listened sooner! I wish I had done it sooner!" That's what my husband and I say all the time, referring, of course, to investing in real estate. It wasn't as if Fred did not tell me to do it every chance he could. I just thought, "I am not a real estate investor." Well, guess what: I am now! And so are a few of our soccer dad friends, our next-door neighbors, and our financial advisor. Investing in residential real estate is one of the best decisions we ever made for our future and for the future of our clients. If you are a real estate agent and you are not encouraging, educating, and leading your clients to start their own real estate investment business, you are missing a huge opportunity... and so are they. You invest a small amount of money into a home purchase and then you have other people move in and they pay off the mortgage for you. Tada! No, really, that's it. In 15 years you now have an asset all paid off. And then guess what: you and they do it again, and again, and again. Any chance you can. READ THIS BOOK. If you can't have Fred with you pestering you daily to do this, the book is the next best thing. It will teach you all you need to know to add this revenue stream to your real estate business. Your clients will thank you for sharing your knowledge and insight and opening their eyes to this additional path to wealth. And what do you get out of it—10, maybe 20 more sales per year? Win-Win. Love it when that happens. BUY THE BOOK!

Mamie Jackson
Berkshire Hathaway Ambassador Real Estate

Fred Tichauer and I share many of the same traits: drive, determination, loyalty, responsibility, and a hardcore work ethic. He has changed my life in ways that otherwise would not have happened.

Fred sold me the home I live in, a foreclosure that my wife and I renovated and in which we are raising our family. He helped me acquire investment properties, and he motivated me to obtain my real estate license. He has imparted upon me his many years of real estate knowledge, which goes far beyond "Here is a great house to buy." It extends to "Here is the president of a bank" (a friend of Fred's), "Here is a contractor" (a friend of Fred's), "Here is an attorney" (a friend of Fred's), and the list goes on. This doesn't happen just by having a license or having some money to buy a house. It happens because Fred believes in himself and his capabilities, and his belief affects everyone around him.

Fred has taken a great step in writing this book and sharing some of his real estate knowledge. What he has to say will rival anything that has been said about real estate previously, but the most important aspect of this book is that Fred has given a piece of himself. The steps involved in buying a property or becoming financially secure are secondary. Having a friend like Fred who makes you believe in YOUR capabilities far outweighs information about what's on a purchase agreement.

Ultimately, Fred would say "First you must believe in yourself" before true success can be achieved. I'm fortunate to have Fred as my best friend. Now you have him through this book.

Shawn Prouse
Owner, Capture Pictures (Broadcast Media)
Investor and Realtor, Berkshire Hathaway HomeServices
Ambassador Real Estate

Fred has been an agent here for a number of years. His wisdom, understanding, and experience of "How to help investors prepare for their future" is second to none. He facilitates a number of different classes for other agents so they can clearly understand how to communicate to their clients the value of buying investment properties. He has a gift. His presentations and ideas are brilliant! Fred's knowledge of the investment process and passion to help others is what makes him a special person. Rarely do you find an individual so willing to openly share what they have learned so they can help others. Fred's book is a must-read.

Vince Leisey
President/Broker
Berkshire Hathaway HomeServices Ambassador Real Estate

Meeting Fred has changed my life... I wish I would have met him in my 20's. His mentorship took me from an average agent to a successful Realtor who now has the tools to advise people on growing wealth. His passion for the business is infectious. Fred believes in you at all times, even when you doubt yourself. Because of his infinite wisdom, I now own and manage a portfolio of rental properties. Furthermore, I am able to customize strategies for my clients as well. He has played a huge role in my success and more importantly has become a good friend. My family and I can't thank you enough, Fred!

Rusty Johnson
Berkshire Hathaway HomeServices Ambassador Real Estate

Coming from a family who owned lots of rental properties, I found myself always saying I didn't want to own any properties myself. After speaking with and having a chance to learn from Fred, I have since changed my outlook on owning additional properties and see how it can help me achieve the financial freedom I have been looking for. I currently own 4 rental properties and plan on adding more to my family's portfolio, I am grateful for the time and energy Fred has given to help me with this journey.

Heather Bullard-Hanika
Managing Broker
Berkshire Hathaway HomeServices

Owning real estate is one of the best ways to build long-term wealth, yet many people don't have any idea how to start investing in real estate for their own future. Fred Tichauer is a true master in real estate ivesting and shares his wisdom in easy-to-understand, and more importantly, easy-to-follow investment strategies. One of the kindest, most focused and professional real estate professionals I have ever met, Fred has built his investment empire, and now he wants to help you build yours!"

— Bob Watson, CRB, CIPS
Global Real Estate Leader

FLIP OR **HOLD**
THE ROAD TO GOLD

A TREASURE MAP TO REAL
ESTATE INVESTMENT RICHES
FOR NEW INVESTORS

FRED TICHAUER

FTCW
PC
Omaha, Nebraska

www.FredTichauer.com

First Edition: August 2021

Paperback: 978-1-7375371-1-3
Mobi: 978-1-7375371-2-0
Library of Congress Data on file with the publisher.

Printed in the United States of America.
10 9 8 7 6 5 4 3 2 1

This book is dedicated to my children,
Kelly, Randi, and Ryan, and to the memory of my parents,
Walter and Helena Tichauer.

CONTENTS

PREFACE

As I started thinking about what I could say in this book on "buy and hold or flip" that has not been said in thousands of other books and articles, it became evident that the task would not be easy. What should I include, what should I leave out, what is essential to know, and what is nice but not necessary to know?

On any given day you can find thousands of books and articles on flipping homes and investing in real estate. Anyone can write an article or a book on real estate investment, even if they have been doing this for only a year or two. If they are good marketers and are convincing, these self-proclaimed "experts" can develop a following. Unfortunately, their recommendations can also drive people to financial ruin.

If you are looking for practical advice, it's important to find a mentor who has a consistent track record and years of experience. That person may not have a high profile. Speaking for myself, I have always been more comfortable operating under the radar.

I see no need to brag about myself or let everyone know how many properties I own or how much money I make. However, I am proud to tell anyone that real estate has treated me very well.

You will not find theories or exaggerations in this book. Instead, I will share practical knowledge and proven ideas that have worked for me for more than 45 years as an investor.

Are you addicted to HGTV? I am not, but occasionally I enjoy watching. Still, these shows bother me as a real estate agent because there is way too much drama, they are not real, and you can predict what the outcome will be. They mention what the buyers paid for the property, but I suspect that the information is not truthful. Also, in determining the profit they never consider interest, taxes, holding cost, etc. What amazes me most is that they sell a property without even having a purchase agreement. Watching these shows also gives people unrealistic expectations for construction timelines. Have you ever seen that amount of work done the day before the open house in a real-life situation? On these shows, they do about two weeks' worth of work in 24 hours. Ridiculous.

There are no secrets in this business that would justify paying $10,000 or more for a system or even hiring an investment coach. This is not rocket science, and you can find information on the Internet for free. If you are creditworthy, a fantastic opportunity awaits you, and you would be better off using your hard-earned money as a down payment or for fix-up costs.

ARE YOU CREDITWORTHY?

You may or may not know your credit score (720 to 850 is considered excellent), but your credit score is only part of the picture. I asked a banker, Leslie Volk, to describe what she looks for in a loan applicant. This is what she said:

It is not easy to precisely define creditworthy based on ratios or credit scores because these measures do not consider how a person will get by when finances are rough. Vacancies and property improvements will need to be covered by the property owner's own resources.

The critical factors in my mind are liquidity and total debt:

How much cash can the borrower get their hands on quickly when needed? Cash balances should be enough to cover at least two to three months of expenses.

Do they have too much total debt to support themselves and the rental property if life takes a turn? Borrowers should have minimal credit card debt.

Good equity in their home can be a source of cash through home equity or refinance, or they can sell the rental property if needed and come out whole.

Saving money for retirement shows discipline, and these funds also can be tapped for liquidity if needed.

If you have good credit, access to money, and a solid financial statement, buying houses to flip or rent out can create wealth, retirement income, and financial freedom. It has worked for me, and it can work for you as well.

When you compare real estate investment to other small businesses, a real estate business is much more likely to succeed. Even under the worst of circumstances, it is impossible to lose all your money in this business. Do you know anyone who lost all their money in a business they owned, especially during COVID-19, through no fault of their own? It breaks my heart to see that happen. In Chapter 2 you'll find out why a real estate investment business is just about foolproof.

When you find a house for sale at a good price in a family-friendly neighborhood, should you fix it up and hold onto it as a long-term rental or make improvements and then flip it to make a profit? This question is the focus of Chapter 1, and the advantages and disadvantages of flipping are described in Chapters 3 and 4.

A word of caution: the current real estate market is highly competitive, making it more challenging than ever to find properties with flipping potential. However, you're likely to find properties that are perfect for the buy-and-hold strategy. I will explain the advantages and disadvantages of the buy-and-hold strategy in Chapters 5 and 6.

You've probably heard that failing to plan is the same as planning to fail. To make sure you will succeed as an investor, I recommend following my Find, Analyze, Buy, Fix, Sell/Rent system (FABFS/R). These five steps are covered in Chapter 7.

How do you figure out whether property A, B, or C will be a good investment? Chapter 8 provides some basic formulas so you won't have to leave things up to chance.

When you decide to flip a property, how much time and money should you put into upgrading it before putting it on the market? Chapter 9 will help you develop a flipping strategy that makes sense for you.

Successful real estate investors work with a knowledgeable agent. I recommend finding a real estate agent in your community who is considered a residential investment specialist, owns rentals, has flipped properties, and understands your local market. The right agent will help you every step of the way, and it will not cost you a cent because they will be your buyer agent. You'll find more on this topic in Chapter 10.

After you decide to buy a property, your next step is to determine how you are going to purchase it—with cash, a line of credit, a conventional loan on the secondary market, or a commercial loan typically amortized over 15 to 20 years with a balloon payment in 5 to 7 years. Obtaining a commercial loan has been my preference because the bank has more flexibility. Chapter 11 describes various financing options so you can decide which one is right for you.

There is a lot of money to be made in this business, and your challenge is to decide how to proceed. Many investors flip some properties and hold on to others. The choice is up to you.

MY BACKGROUND AS AN INVESTOR/AGENT

I have a college degree, but it has nothing to do with real estate. I graduated from the University of Nebraska at Omaha in 1973 with a bachelor's degree in education. (By the way, nobody has ever asked me what my major or grade point average was.)

In the mid-'70s I had little knowledge about real estate but was lucky enough to find a fantastic real estate agent who became my mentor. His name was Jerry Sicuinas. He put me at ease, but I was also smart enough to realize that real estate was an excellent way to add income. I started investing in real estate at age 21 when I purchased a duplex and then moved into one side and rented out the other. I thought it was a cool concept to have somebody else covering most of my monthly mortgage payment. When I sold the duplex three years later (I will fudge a little and call that my first flipping experience), I made enough money to make a down payment on three properties.

My parents were getting older and had no retirement savings. I did not want them to rely solely on Social Security during their golden years, so I helped them buy three rental properties that generated around $1,500 a month in rental income.

At that point, I decided that it might be a good idea to get a license, so in 1980 I enrolled in real estate classes. After failing the test twice, I finally passed on the third try and used my license solely to find, buy, and sell my investment properties while working full-time as an executive with the Boy Scouts of America.

After a successful 24-year career with the BSA, I decided to expand my real estate holdings. In 1998 I began a new career as a full-time real estate agent. I am considered an independent contractor, and I am often asked who I work for. My response is that I work for myself and utilize the resources of the real estate company to help me in my business. Additionally, the values I learned in the BSA, such as honor, trustworthiness, and integrity, have served as my guiding principles in this business.

Today I consider myself to be one of Omaha's most knowledgeable investment property experts. I am not claiming to be #1 or #100, but the expertise I have acquired as an investor has been invaluable for my clients.

I have bought and sold hundreds of properties over the years and still control an extensive rental property portfolio worth a few million dollars that generates a six-figure annual income. In other words, I walk the talk.

You may be wondering by now if I compete with my clients to purchase properties, and the answer is no. However, I have bought quite a few properties when my clients decided to pass up an opportunity for one reason or another. I have also passed up buying hundreds of properties over the years because they did not meet my requirements.

Some people like to brag that they own a hundred or more "doors." Does that mean they own ten apartments of 10 units each or 100 houses? Instead of talking about the number of doors, I prefer to talk about the number of units.

As you'll see in this book, I believe in only buying properties to flip or hold in family-friendly neighborhoods. You will never go wrong if you consider such things as crime rate, school reputation, and whether the house is close to a park, a grocery store, restaurants, and so on.

I have chosen to invest only in houses, duplexes, and small apartments of six units or less. When it is time to execute my exit plan, who would be the likely buyer of a commercial property or a large apartment? It would be another investor, and it's extremely difficult to get two investors to agree on what a property is worth. By contrast, a house is much easier to manage, much simpler to analyze and sell, and the buyer is likely to be easier to work with.

Although it was not in my plans, I have trained hundreds of agents over the years. Quite often, I teach classes and seminars on all aspects of the investment niche market. I provide continuing education classes approved by the Nebraska Real Estate Commission for real estate agents. I also travel all over the country providing classes for brokerage firms. I am proud to say that I have had several real estate agents as clients and that some of my clients have become real estate agents.

My hard work has paid off, and I am enjoying the "American Dream" of financial freedom. Even though I don't have to work, I continue to make a very good living while helping my clients accomplish their definition of financial independence.

How many people are fortunate to continue working because they love what they do? I am just as passionate about this business as I was when I started. I am often asked when I plan on retiring, and my response is "Never." Why would I want to retire when I enjoy what I am doing? I am especially proud to have helped several clients achieve "millionaire investor" status.

SO, WHAT DRIVES ME NOW?

My mission: To help clients from all walks of life generate wealth so they are financially prepared for their "golden years." To strive to always go above and beyond my clients' expectations by being a wealth advisor, coach, mentor, and source of information for all of their investment needs.

My vision: To be the real estate agent of choice for those who want to become financially independent.

My values: To always be 100% honest and never put my own needs before my clients' needs. When they make money, I will make money, so there is no need for me to worry about each commission check.

My legacy: To help real estate agents and clients by sharing my knowledge with them.

If you have been on the fence about investing, I hope this book will motivate you to get started. Be sure to find a qualified agent who can guide you every step of the way (see Chapter 10 for more information). Remember that wealth is found on the other side of fear. If I can do it, so can you.

WHY I WROTE THIS BOOK

I decided to write this book because I am 100 percent certain that for the average individual who is creditworthy and willing to work hard, a real estate business is the most realistic path available for wealth-building, retirement income, and ultimately financial freedom. The bottom line is that when you invest in real estate, you and no one else is in control of your financial future.

Speaking of the future, have you given much thought to your retirement? Are you concerned about whether you will have enough money in your retirement account to maintain your current lifestyle?

Do you have money invested in the stock market? If so, do you understand how the stock market works? Are you in control of the performance of your investment, or is someone else? I hope these thought-provoking questions will motivate you to consider investing in real estate.

My dad made a total of $65,000 from 1963 to 1974. During the 1980s they invested in three rental properties that provided them with $1,500 a month in income. When they sold their properties, the money they made provided them with enough retirement income to live comfortably.

When I was a teenager, I never dreamed that someday I would achieve financial freedom and leave a legacy for my family and my favorite charities. The money I have made from real estate had not been the only reward, as my life has been enriched through lifetime friendships with my clients, tenants, and colleagues.

I think by now you know where I am going with this. Housing has met the test of time and will always be in demand. With a solid business plan and enough suitable properties in family-friendly neighborhoods, you will find that wealth-building, retirement income, and financial freedom are within your reach.

A word of advice—do not try to do this on your own. Find the best Realtor/agent in your community who is a residential investment specialist and hopefully an investor. He or she will be able to guide you every step of the way.

Whatever you do, do not listen to the pundits. This is the real deal, and the sky is the limit.

When you have finished reading this book, I invite you to drop me an email or call me at 402-679-3914 to ask questions or let me know what you thought of the book. My email address is reinvestorsclientsforlife@gmail.com

ACKNOWLEDGMENTS

This book is dedicated to my parents' memory because they were incredible role models who laid a strong foundation for the person I am today.

Early on, I watched them work hard to provide for my brother and me. They taught me that to get ahead, you must make sacrifices, overcome obstacles, and have deep passion and enthusiasm for whatever you are doing. They inspired me to become a high achiever, be unafraid to try new things even if I might fail, be courageous, and help others along the way.

My parents moved from Europe to Montevideo, Uruguay, in South America in the mid-1940s. From a young age, I was aware that they both worked extremely hard and had successful businesses. We had a happy and normal life. They owned a lovely home in a desirable neighborhood as well as a vacation home. Life was good for us, but they became concerned about Uruguay's growing political unrest and decided to emigrate to the United States in 1963 when I was 12 years old. This was one of the most unselfish decisions they could have made, and to this day, I continue to think, "What if?" They came to this country because they wanted us to have the opportunity for a better life.

My parents worked hard for the money they earned. When I remember my dad taking his little metal lunch bucket to work each day, the thought brings tears to my eyes.

My parents instilled in me the drive to not let anything get in my way if I wanted something badly enough. They taught me so many life lessons, yet it took me a long time to realize how much I had learned from them.

They used to tell me, "You have to pay the price to succeed because nothing in life comes easily." I am the product of the American dream—proof that anything is possible in this country if you work hard and are willing to pay the price.

Although I did not understand it at the time, subconsciously, all along, I was telling myself that I would never rely on anyone else for my financial future, and someday I would become financially independent.

In addition to my parents, another individual who inspired me to achieve was a family member who predicted that I would probably end up in jail and not amount to much. I was not a juvenile delinquent; I just got into trouble at school often. I had a chair reserved for me in the principal's and counselor's offices because I visited them regularly.

When I came to this country at 12 years old, I was scared to death and did not speak English. I wanted attention, so I became the class clown. When I was in eighth grade, the principal told my mother and this relative that I would be kicked out of school the next time I got into trouble. That got my attention.

I was aware that this family member had told my parents that I would end up in jail and not amount to much, and her prediction ended up having a significant impact on my life because I did not want her to be able to tell my parents, "I told you so."

I used this negative chapter in my life to challenge myself and focus. Even in my adult life, I never thanked this individual for helping me. I wanted so badly to prove she was wrong about me that it inspired me to succeed. I turned a negative into a positive. I also know that I would never have gone to college if I had not earned a football scholarship to the University of Nebraska at Omaha. I was one of the original soccer-style kickers in the state of Nebraska going back to junior high school days. My message to you is if you have had an adverse event in your life, use it as your motivation to quietly prove people wrong.

During my years as an investor, a lot of people have helped me along the way. Where would I be without them? Some people proudly say they are self-made, but I'm sure they had mentors who do not get the credit they deserve.

First and foremost, I am thankful for the relationships and help I have received from Security National Bank in Omaha. They believed in me and loaned me the money to make my purchases when I was asset poor. This has been a 40-plus-year relationship. If they had not believed in me, then investing in real estate would have been nothing more than a dream. I know that some people shop around to save ¼% on their loan, but to me it is much more critical to work with a bank that will have my back in a time of need.

Many people have inspired me and had so much influence on my real estate career that it would be impossible to thank each of them individually. One person who comes to mind immediately is Jerry Sicuinas, the real estate agent who helped me buy my first duplex in 1973. Jerry ignited my lifelong passion for real estate investing.

I am grateful to Jacob Scott Hanika and Liz Kelly for providing feedback that helped me improve this book.

Thank you to my editor, Janet Tilden, for her sharp eye and skill in polishing my words.

Finally, I want to thank my children, Kelly, Randi, and Ryan, for their support, encouragement, and belief in me. I am incredibly grateful that my daughter Kelly has joined me as a partner in my real estate practice.

CHAPTER 1
SHOULD I BUY AND HOLD OR BUY AND FLIP?

Affirmation for Today

- *I am grateful for all the good coming my way, counting my blessings, and continuously reminding myself that anything I want in life is up to me because everyone else has their own dreams and aspirations.*
- *I am blessed to have good health, a wonderful family, and friends. I am wealthy in so many ways.*
- *I can finally look at my finances without fear because I am financially free, and my income exceeds my expenses. It feels great, and this is only the beginning. Look out: I am coming in strong!*
- *I will finally live the life I always envisioned. I will never forget where I came from, and when it is time to retire it will be on my terms.*
- *I have nothing to complain about. For those who are less fortunate than I am, I wish them everything good because they also deserve to live the life they have always dreamed about.*
- *I earned everything that is coming my way through a tried-and-true method—HARD WORK.*

When you invest your hard-earned money, you should have a purpose in mind. What is your purpose?

That may sound like a dumb question. For retirement, right?

Are you on track in saving money for retirement? Have you even started setting aside money for the future? If not, I promise you that someday you will be old like me. Retirement planning should not be left up to chance, and the sooner you start planning, the better able you will be to answer the "what if" question. Will you be able to retire on your own terms or just retire?

So, going back to my original question, what is your purpose for investing? Mine was always to create additional income streams and achieve financial freedom. Don't get me wrong. I think it's great that I can count on my retirement income from the Boy Scouts of America and Social Security, but I see them as a bonus rather than a primary source of income.

Will you have any additional income streams after you retire? Are you in control of your investments, or is someone else?

I realized very early on that real estate was going to be my path to wealth. My decision to invest in real estate has been life-changing, and it can be for you as well.

Where and how you invest your money is your business. Are you in charge of your financial future, or is someone else? No one should or could care more about your finances than you do. Decisions, decisions, decisions. Make the right decision—you deserve it!

IS IT BETTER TO BUY AND HOLD OR BUY AND FLIP?

Have you ever flipped a property or owned a rental? If the answer is yes, congratulations! If not, then you might be wondering how to decide whether to buy a residential property and use it as a rental or renovate and sell it at a higher price (flip).

"Should I buy and hold or buy and flip?" is a great question, but it has no right or wrong answer. The right answer for you will depend on whether you want to create wealth or make a living.

Shows on HGTV have made the process of flipping seem effortless. You find a cheap property, put some money and sweat equity into fixing it up, and then sell it for a considerable profit or rent it out.

Experienced real estate investors can indeed make enormous profits by flipping properties or by keeping them as rentals, because ultimately the tenant is the one who is paying down the mortgage. If you have thought about flipping but never pulled the trigger, now is the time to do it. If you have dabbled in real estate unsuccessfully in the past, now is the time to get re-engaged.

How can you get started? Unfortunately, you're likely to encounter a lot of conflicting information on flipping. If you Google "flip houses," you'll get millions of hits. (I am not exaggerating.) No wonder people are confused.

Do not get me started with all the "free" seminars advertised on TV. There is no reason to spend thousands of dollars for reams of paper that will end up on a shelf or on eBay.

If you're new to real estate investment, your first step should be to find a real estate agent who specializes in residential investing and understands your local market. Interview a few agents who have the background you deserve and can guide you every step of the way, then pick the one you like best.

> Find a real estate agent who has investment experience

Working with a real estate investment specialist will not cost you a dime because they are serving as your buyer agent. Instead of spending your money on books and seminars, you can use it for a down payment or fix-up costs.

If flipping interests you, I recommend that you go for it. It has been extraordinarily lucrative for me, so I find it easy to understand why more and more people want to get in the game.

Today's real estate market is completely different from what it was like as recently as five years ago. It has become much harder to find properties with flipping potential. In my home city of Omaha, Nebraska, the number of residential property listings has dropped dramatically in recent years. The inventory of homes for sale in Douglas County, Nebraska, in December 2018 was 1,271. Two years later it had dropped to 562, and on March 31, 2021, it was 329.

Why is the housing market so competitive, especially for properties in the $100,000 to $200,000 range? Because investors are buying properties, and first-time home buyers cannot compete with cash offers.

The scarcity of properties for sale is making it harder than ever to find good deals. That's one reason you need to have the right agent on your side. An experienced agent will understand your local market and know when a good deal comes up, maybe even before it gets listed. On a positive note, the scarcity of properties also means that the selling price will be higher after a property is improved.

Today's increasingly competitive environment proves that real estate is one of the best options for hardworking people to make a good living, build wealth, earn retirement income, and ultimately achieve financial freedom.

> The demand for properties is at an all-time high

It is still a great time to start building wealth by purchasing income-producing properties or flipping to make extra cash. In Omaha, Nebraska, I made an average of $15,000 to $30,000 personally on each flip before taxes, and some of my clients make significantly more. In your area the profits may be much higher. I have a client who has flipped over 300 properties to date and in one year made over $300,000.

I started flipping properties in the 1980s before the term "flipping" was widely used. How times have changed! Flipping has been an enormous part of my income, so I understand the ins and outs of this game. Keep in mind that I did not do any of the remodeling work myself.

In late 2017 I bought a duplex because it had a five-car garage that I wanted to use for storage. I was hoping the city would allow me to get a separate legal description for the garages and sell the duplex. Unfortunately, my request was turned down. I did not want another rental because I already had plenty, so I sold it in 2018 and made $90,000 in a few months.

In late 2020, I purchased two houses for a total of $145,000 (one for $90,000 and the other for $55,000). The $90,000 property required $40,000 in renovation costs, and I sold for $198,500. I kept the $55,000 property, and it currently rents for $840 per month. It has a two-car garage bigger than the house, and I am using the garage for storage.

I have continued to flip properties for ordinary income and rely on my sizable rental portfolio for wealth building and retirement income. Real estate investors often have strong opinions about whether it is better to flip or to buy and hold, but both strategies can produce excellent results. The right strategy is the one that will fulfill your needs.

Have you talked with anyone lately who is not a fan of real estate? What was their opinion on flipping or long-term rentals? If they tried one of these strategies and it did not work well for them, perhaps they made a poor decision or worked with a real estate agent who lacked experience with investment properties. Or maybe they were speculators rather than investors. Did they have a business plan? Did they pay too much to purchase a property or remodel it and end up losing money? Investors can minimize risk by following a business plan and making their money when they buy.

Flipping is like being an artist who takes a blank canvas and creates a beautiful picture. You can get a lot of satisfaction from reconditioning a rundown property and helping to improve a neighborhood. Even more rewarding is the fact that you are making the dream of homeownership possible for a family and, at the same time, earning a nice profit. It is an example of the Win-Win concept at work.

> Flipping benefits the seller, the buyer, and the neighborhood

Some people use the profits from flipping to buy a new car, pay off credit card debt, put their children or grandchildren through college, or take a vacation. Flipping is a terrific way to earn money in a short period of time, while buying and owning rental properties is the path to building wealth for the future. Either of these options is certainly better than doing nothing at all.

I think doing some of both is the best way to go—flipping for ordinary income and holding long-term rentals to build wealth. Incidentally, I do not believe in using the profits from a flip to purchase another property that you intend on flipping. A better option is to refinance the property and try to pull out most of your investment. If you decide not to hold onto it as a long-term rental, I recommend keeping it for at least a year because of the tax advantages (see the explanation below). A 1031 exchange (described in Chapter 5) will allow you to use 100% of the profit and defer taxes on it.

The main distinction between flipping and holding is how you will be taxed. Of course the IRS will want you to hand over some of the money you make.

There are two types of capital gains, and they are treated differently for tax purposes. If you hold a property for one year or less, the profits will be considered a short-term gain and taxed the same way as ordinary income. If you hold a property for more than one year, it will be considered a long-term gain and taxed at a lower rate.

For details on capital gains tax rates, consult your accountant for further information.

Real estate has met the test of time, and housing will always be a necessity. Owning a real estate investment business provides many perks. Whether you choose to buy and hold or buy and flip, taking either path is much better than sitting on the sidelines.

CHAPTER 2
THE BEST SMALL BUSINESS, HANDS DOWN

Have you ever thought about starting your own business? If so, you are not alone. According to the U.S. Small Business Administration, there are 31.7 million small businesses in the United States. Unfortunately, 20% of small businesses fail within their first year. By the end of their fifth year, roughly 50% have shut down. After ten years, only a third have survived.

I am sure you know at least one person who had a great idea for a business. They refinanced their residence or used collateral to borrow money to get started, only to have their business fail. They may have lost everything and had to file for bankruptcy.

When people work for someone else, they may be making a living, but are they creating wealth? What about their employer? Is he or she creating wealth or barely making a living also?

I think you know where I am going with this, and I hope that by the time you are done reading this book, you will agree with me that real estate is a much better option than any other small business.

There are many reasons why small businesses fail, but a few are always at the top of the list: insufficient capital, poor management, inadequate business planning, overblown marketing budgets, lack of demand, and cash flow problems.

82% of new business failures involve cash flow problems

When I was doing my research for this book, it broke my heart to find out that 60% of restaurants do not make it past their first year and 80% go out of business within five years.

How many small businesses in your community have had to close their doors? Turning an idea into a lucrative business is never easy, but it is particularly challenging for small businesses.

Why do so many new businesses fail? In my opinion, the underlying cause is often a lack of planning. Before starting a business, you need to ask yourself the following questions:

1. *Is this business likely to succeed over the long term?* Real estate has met the test of time, and housing will always be a necessity.

2. *Is it a killer idea?* Real estate has met the test of time, and housing will always be a necessity.

3. *Does it solve a problem?* Real estate has met the test of time, and housing will always be a necessity.

4. *Does it fulfill a need?* Real estate has met the test of time, and housing will always be a necessity.

5. *Does it offer something the market wants?* Real estate has met the test of time, and housing will always be a necessity.

Having said all of this, I think it is only fair to consider why a real estate investment business could fail. Let me start by saying that real estate is just about foolproof, and I have never met anyone who has failed in this business. (Yes, it is a business that is worth owning that will keep on giving and giving.) However, I can think of several reasons why a real estate investor could fail:

1. Making poor investment choices such as buying properties in high-crime areas.

2. Not interviewing agents to see who is most qualified to explain the advantages and disadvantages of various real estate options.

3. Not having a good reason to invest in the first place. I call this the *Big Why*. Your motivation should be to build wealth and earn retirement income, not just generate cash flow with no goal in mind.

4. Not having a business plan to direct their buying decisions. (A sample business plan is provided in the Resources section at the end of this book.)

5. Falling in love with the property instead of the deal and not taking the time to figure out whether the property will be a good investment.

6. Overleveraging properties by putting no money down or making a very small down payment. (Why would anyone sell a good property for no money down?)

7. Buying lots of "junk" properties instead of owning enough of the "right" properties.

8. Constantly refinancing properties instead of paying some of them off. I understand that building a portfolio is necessary, but at some point paying them off should be your goal. If you have little or no equity, you have no protection if anything goes wrong.

9. Collecting rent and not making the mortgage payment. You may have trouble believing that anyone would do this, but I listed a few investment properties from a local bank where this happened.

10. Not maintaining the property. Why would anyone invest their hard-earned money to buy a property, only to let it get rundown by not making repairs?

11. Poor tenant selection through lack of proper due diligence. An example is renting to someone who wants to pay cash for the first month's rent and security deposit and needs to move

in today. How many people have a couple of thousand dollars in cash? I would be suspicious of their business model.

12. Not inspecting each property at least quarterly. If you don't find problems and fix them quickly, they could end up costing you thousands of dollars.

13. Not doing proper due diligence such as having an investor/ home inspection or a sewer/plumber inspection before purchasing a property. (What is the difference between a home inspection and an investor inspection? An investor inspection checks the major components such as HVAC, roof, attic, foundation, etc.)

Now that I have listed a few reasons why a real estate investment business might not succeed, it's time to explain why I believe a real estate investment business is a winner:

1. Housing (shelter) will always be a necessity. It has met the test of time and will continue to be one of the most reliable ways to create wealth and generate retirement income.

2. Unlike traditional businesses, it is just about impossible to lose all the money you have invested in real estate even if a property must be sold quickly. Keep in mind that a savvy investor always buys undervalued properties.

3. This business can be done on a part-time basis.

4. Your real estate investments work for you 24/7 because tenants pay rent even if there are outside influences such as a blizzard. A traditional business that cannot open its doors for any reason must still pay rent and other expenses despite having no income on the days they are closed.

5. Properties in desirable areas will always be in demand and will continue to appreciate. Even if a property maintains the

value of its original purchase price, you are still better off owning it than not owning it.

6. There is no real overhead as long as the property is rented. Your investment business can be run from your kitchen table using your smartphone and computer.

7. You can operate the business without hiring employees until you have so many properties that you need help. Property managers, electricians, plumbers, drywall installers, roofers, and other specialists are independent contractors. Others on the team, such as your attorney, accountant, title company, termite inspector, and home inspector, are only utilized as needed.

8. During times of inflation, property values and rent also tend to increase. When taxes, insurance, and other expenses go up, you can pass them down to the tenant in the form of rent increases.

9. Even if the real estate market goes south, a savvy investor who purchased undervalued properties is well protected. Ultimately fluctuations in property values are unimportant if the properties are being used as long-term rentals, since the tenant is making the mortgage payment.

10. In addition to the long-term rental model, a real estate business can include wholesaling to other investors or "flipping" to owner-occupied buyers.

11. The 1031 Tax-Deferred Exchange is only available to real estate investors. It allows you to sell a property for a profit and defer capital gains taxes in the sale year. This can be done repeatedly, and it is a terrific way to grow your portfolio.

12. Tenants pay down the debt, and as properties are paid off the investor has a higher net worth.

With a solid business plan and the right team in place, real estate is a winning proposition. The biggest roadblocks for most would-be investors are never getting started and trying to "go it alone" without any guidance.

The demand for housing will never go away

More and more people are investing their hard-earned money in real estate. Real estate is the best investment available, according to Gallup's annual Economy and Finance survey conducted in April 2020. Interest in stock and mutual fund investing has fallen to its lowest level since 2012. By contrast, real estate has been the top investment choice since 2016.

My business model is simple: Buy undervalued property that has flipping or long-term investment potential. If you are going to rent it, do not be in a rush to rent it to the first person who can pay you the first month's rent and security deposit, especially if they want to pay in cash. If you take time for due diligence and they qualify, you have a tenant. You collect rent, make the mortgage payments, maintain the property, and the money left over is cash flow that is yours to spend.

I am 100% certain that most people can understand the model of a real estate investment business and follow it. By contrast, few people understand how the stock market works. Another big consideration is that when you invest in stocks you are not in control. With real estate I am in control; I can touch, feel, drive by the property, make improvements, raise the rent, and so on. In addition, what happens globally impacts the stock market but has no bearing on my properties because real estate is local.

Think about how powerful this business can be for you and others. How many people do you know who are earning at least $200 in dividends every month from their current investments? You can easily get that amount of cash flow with only one rental.

In my 45-plus years as an investor and more than 20 years as a Realtor, I cannot recall anyone who had to close their real estate investment business due to lack of demand. Housing will always be a necessity. If the tenant pays rent and the mortgage payment is being made, the property is well maintained, and there is money left over every month (cash flow) to make repairs, you have a successful business model. Just starting with one property and building along the way can allow you to obtain a sizable portfolio worth several million dollars, generating a six-figure income. It's a winning proposition.

> I am proud to have helped several clients achieve "millionaire investor" status

According to Global Wealth Report, the total number of millionaires in the United States in 2020 was 18.6 million, with 675,000 new millionaires added from 2018 to 2019 alone.

Do not ever let the pundits tell you that you cannot become a millionaire from real estate investment. I have helped several clients in Omaha, Nebraska, achieve "millionaire investor" status. If you are hard-working and creditworthy, this is a great business that is within your reach.

SEVEN KEYS TO BECOMING A MILLIONAIRE REAL ESTATE INVESTOR

1. Use the assistance of the right real estate agent who is also an investor and can guide you every step of the way.

2. Develop a business plan and evaluate your progress at least annually.

3. Save 10 to 15 percent of each paycheck until you can make a down payment on another property, and repeat.

4. Live below your means. Before making a purchase, ask yourself, "Do I need this?" What you need is real estate to support your lifestyle in retirement.

5. Don't use credit cards. (If you do use them, pay off balances monthly.)

6. Let your money work hard for you instead of working hard for your money. Making a lot of money generally does not create wealth. It allows you to make a nice living. (In today's world, there is no longer such a thing as job security.)

7. Start your own real estate business, and you will be glad you did.

If you're thinking about owning long-term rental property, the outlook is excellent. According to the Pew Research Center, the total number of U.S. households grew by 7.6 million over the past decade. However, the number of households headed by owners remained relatively flat, while households headed by renters grew by nearly 10 percent during the same period (Pew Research).

Rising home prices, lingering fears from the housing crash, and large amounts of student debt are some of the reasons why many Americans choose to rent instead of buy. Many young adults have not accumulated enough savings to make a down payment on a house. Also, owning a home inhibits moving, and young adults move more frequently than any other age group. As a result, they may prefer not to become homeowners while they're in their twenties (Pew Research).

The opportunities for anyone looking to build wealth through real estate investing are endless:

- The number of housing units in the U.S. currently is 136.57 million (U.S. Census Bureau, 2018).
- 36.6% of housing units are occupied by renters, and 63.4% are owner-occupied (U.S. Census Bureau. 2018).

Clearly, buying residential property to hold or flip is a winning proposition. Few business opportunities have a lower cost of entry or a higher income potential than real estate. This industry has met the test of time, and the demand from home buyers and renters will always exist because housing will continue to be a necessity.

While there are many real estate options available to you, including houses, apartment buildings, commercial buildings, business and industrial parks, storage units, etc., my expertise falls in the residential investment niche market. I would highly recommend you do the same. Are you aware that a fourplex or less is residential, just like a house? A terrific way for someone to get started is to live in one unit and rent the other three out. There is some debate as to whether you can depreciate the entire fourplex and deduct the operating expenses if you live in one of the units and pay yourself market rent. Some CPAs say yes, and others say no. I guess this is an example of an opinion. Make sure to seek the advice of a qualified tax advisor.

CHAPTER 3
ADVANTAGES OF FLIPPING

Newcomers to real estate investing often ask me whether it's better to flip properties or to buy and hold. My answer is always the same: "It depends on why you are doing this in the first place." I call this the *Big Why: What are you hoping to accomplish by investing in real estate?*

Many people tell me they want to flip so they can make enough money to buy another property. After I mention that the profits from flipping are likely to be treated as ordinary income for tax purposes, they realize that this might not be the best strategy for them. (See Chapter 5 for more information.)

I can say with 100% certainty that both flipping and holding are much better than sitting on the sidelines while others reap the benefits of this fantastic industry.

Properties are available on any given day at every price point. Take some time to evaluate the pluses and minuses before deciding whether to buy and flip or to buy and hold. No matter which path you choose, it should meet the requirements of your Big Why, which should be wealth building, retirement income, and financial freedom.

Below are some of the advantages of flipping. Perhaps you can think of others.

1. A nice profit can be made in a relatively short period of time. The key to success is not to overpay for the property or underestimate the amount of work required to prepare it for sale. It is critical to stay on budget and to complete the project on schedule. Most projects can be completed within three to six weeks. One of the primary reasons people get in trouble is that they have no clue how long the project is going to take.

2. You are your own boss, and you will reap the financial rewards of good decisions. If flipping is done correctly, it can easily replace your income from the workplace.

3. For people who are in another line of work, flipping can provide an additional source of income and an opportunity to partner with someone so that both of you can enjoy the benefits.

4. Flipping is an amazing option for anyone who is creditworthy and has a solid financial statement.

5. Each time you flip a property, you will increase your knowledge of this industry. In the future you will have a much better idea of what to buy and what to walk away from. While there are deals to be had on any given day, you must be careful to follow two rules: (1) always fall in love with the deal and not the property, and (2) remember that you make your money when you buy. These two simple rules will be your safety net if you encounter some unforeseen costs, but with the due diligence of investor inspection (a slightly modified traditional home inspection that only checks the big-ticket items), sewer inspection, and an understanding of contractor cost and the cost of supplies, you should have everything well covered.

6. Flipping is much safer than investing in the stock market because you are in control of your investment. Real estate is localized, and what happens in other cities has no bearing on what happens in your city. Additionally, your money is tied up for only a short period, further minimizing your risk.

7. 7. When you flip a property, there are no tenants to deal with. I have seen experienced and inexperienced investors skip the due diligence required for tenant selection and

regret this omission after the property is trashed.

8. 8.   You can make a six-figure income even on a part-time basis. (The current real estate market is so competitive that it is critical to have the right agent on your side.)

9. 9.   You can have the satisfaction of making it possible for people to buy a nice home at a good price. One of my greatest joys is finding a rundown property in a family-friendly neighborhood, making the necessary updates, and selling it for a nice profit. Often the buyer's agent will tell me that the buyers are literally in tears because they had never thought they could afford to buy such a nice house.

10. 10. You can gain experience without making a long-term commitment, and if you decide to do it again, it pretty much becomes a push-button experience. You will have a relatively good idea of the cost of materials such as paint, flooring, kitchen and bathroom cabinets, as well as how much an electrician, plumber, and HVAC contractor will charge, so there should be no surprises.

Your first flip is likely to feel scary and nerve-wracking because of your fear of the unknown. Choosing a Realtor who is an experienced flipper will help you avoid pitfalls.

The mistakes I see most often are not having an experienced Realtor and not having the property inspected. I have been amazed to witness the number of buyers who are unwilling to pay for simple inspections that could save them thousands of dollars. They think they know it all, only to find out later that the sewer line is shot and they will have to spend a good chunk of their profit to replace it.

ATTOM Data Solutions reports that in 2019, the number of homes flipped hit an **8-year market share high,** accounting for 6.2% of all home sales in the nation. A total of 245,864 U.S. single-family homes were flipped in 2019.

It is unnecessary to buy expensive supplies when you are remodeling a house. Instead, look for discontinued or discounted items of good quality. Your goal should be to turn out a superior product and gain a reputation in your community as someone who cares. Taking shortcuts and hiding problems will come back to bite you later.

Keep in mind that most buyers will do a home inspection, sewer inspection, and possibly a radon test, so there is no reason to hide something. Hiding things only ruins your reputation. Remember that flipping is all about win-win.

Flipping is one of the less risky options in terms of the initial investment. Additionally, there are fewer issues and minimal carrying costs since most of the properties with flipping potential are in the distressed category, so the initial investment will likely be lower than the market price.

How hard is it to make $1,000,000 over time from flipping? It is not as hard as you might think if you are realistic and have a real estate agent with the knowledge and experience you deserve.

How many houses would you need to flip to earn a million dollars in profit? It depends on the price point.

1. Flip 1: $1,000,000

2. Flip 4: $250,000

3. Flip 10: $100,000

4. Flip 20: $50,000

5. Flip 33: $33,333

6. Flip 50: $20,000

Most flippers make their money from options 4, 5, or 6 (at least in Omaha, Nebraska). Can you imagine the amount of risk involved in options 1, 2, and 3?

Talk about risk—I know someone who paid over $600,000 for a property in 2018. It was listed in January 2019 for around $1,500,000. I have no idea how much money they spent on the renovation, but can you imagine the consequences of making a poor decision when the stakes are so high? There is no room for error, so flipping at a high-end home should only be done by experienced investors or contractors who know what they are doing. The lesson here is this: Stick to what you know.

Real estate is very forgiving up to a point, and most of my clients buy properties to flip in the $100,000 to 150,000 price range. Why? Because buyers don't expect the workmanship to be 100% perfect in a moderately priced home. The opposite is true in the high-end market where every detail matters. I would not even think about touching such a property, despite the potential to make hundreds of thousands of dollars from a single flip.

Chapter 8 covers what I call the safety net and explains how you can get peace of mind by using a "good, better, best scenario" to make decisions instead of going in blindly and hoping for the best. I am aware that the pundits say real estate investment is risky and that you could lose a lot of money. I made a minimum of $20,000 on each flip and as much as $90,000 on two different occasions. I have established an excellent track record with the over 150 flips that I did, and I am confident that flipping can be an additional source of income for you as well.

Keep in mind that I did not do any of the renovation work myself, but I still made plenty of profit on every flip. If I can do it, so can you.

CHAPTER 4
DISADVANTAGES OF FLIPPING

Some people say that flipping is risky, but I have found that the risk is minimal if you do your due diligence before purchasing the property. The inspection will uncover any problems so you can make an informed decision.

If you buy a property at the right price, know what the expenses will be, and understand what the minimum sale price is likely to be, the process of buying and flipping is just about foolproof.

Some will say that a disadvantage of flipping is the risk of losing money, but any worthwhile venture involves some risk. No risk, no reward. Money can be found on the other side of fear. You can minimize your risk and increase your chances of success by working with the right agent who can help you figure out the anticipated expenses so you can purchase the property at a price that makes sense. Your agent can help you explore various scenarios so you can see whether you are likely to make the desired profit from buying and flipping a specific property.

I believe the benefits of flipping far outweigh any disadvantages, and I would strongly recommend it to anyone who wants to make extra money or use it as an ongoing business venture.

In addition to selling a property on the open market, you can convert a property to a rental, so there is no real risk involved. Remember that even a person who makes a poor decision will never lose all of their investment because housing will always be worth something.

I don't spend much time thinking about the potential disadvantages of flipping because I see money signs when a property sells. However, let's take a look at the so-called disadvantages of flipping:

1. If you're not careful, you could end up paying too much money to the IRS at tax time. Navigating self-employment tax and IRS rules about house flipping can be tricky, so it makes sense to work with a competent and knowledgeable accountant. Do you have an accountant who has owned rentals or flipped properties? If not, you need to find an accountant who has expertise in this industry.

2. Holding costs can cut into your profit. The cost of utilities, taxes, insurance, yard maintenance, snow removal, and so on should be considered. The longer it takes to complete the renovation, the more expenses you will incur. Interest is the biggest expense if you borrow money to buy the property. (I will cover how to use a line of credit to buy properties in Chapter 6.) Have you ever noticed that flipping shows on HGTV generally do not talk much about holding costs and the fact that they add up quickly?

3. Poor workmanship can cost you a sale. With instant access to the Internet, buyers are savvier than ever about what to look for in a quality home. If you skimp on upgrades and repairs, the property is likely to sit on the market for months and months, waiting for a buyer who will not mind paying for substandard quality.

   Cutting corners is one of the biggest blunders anyone can make. The higher the price point, the more sophisticated the buyer will be. However, there is no room for shoddy workmanship at any price point. Your reputation will follow you, and I am sure you would rather be known as someone who turns out a good product than the opposite.

   I have seen way too many flips that are an embarrassment due to poor workmanship, such as ceramic tiles where the pattern does not line up or vinyl plank flooring that is not installed properly. When buyers notice sloppy workmanship, they are less likely to write an offer and more likely to spot other imperfections that they might otherwise have overlooked—or worse, skip a showing altogether due to other properties of yours that they've seen before.

How many times have you been to a house where the doorknobs and hinges are painted, or some are replaced with brushed nickel while others are brass? Is that a big red flag and a turnoff? It will indicate to a prospective buyer that you are likely to be skimping on other things. Mentally they are preparing to get the heck out of there.

What is the point of upgrading a kitchen if the countertops or tile work is subpar? You get what you pay for, and it is crucial to work with an all-around contractor rather than hire a different contractor for every job.

I generally deal with houses priced in the mid-150Ks, and buyers at that price point are generally not expecting new windows; however, they do expect quality workmanship and windows that are not painted shut. On the other hand, when a house has lots of little imperfections that are noticeable, windows may become an issue.

The first thing a prospective buyer will notice is the front door. Is it in good condition or painted in an accent color that is pleasing? Or is the front door in bad shape or sloppily painted? What about the garage door? Is it in good repair? Does it go up and down easily? Don't overlook the trim or weather stripping.

Not paying attention to the heating and cooling system is one of the most significant blunders people make. They do an excellent job of updating the house but fail to replace a furnace or central air conditioner that is 20-plus years old. Their logic is that they will pay for a home warranty. I can assure you that the furnace and AC will be one of the most significant sticking points after the home inspection has been completed. It is better to replace these items before the house is listed, because the longer the property remains on the market the less profit you are going to make.

Another big error is failing to upgrade an outdated electrical system. An electrical service panel that has fuses should be replaced with one that has circuit breakers. One of the most significant issues with many service panels is double-tapping (two wires connected to a circuit breaker that is designed for one wire) or failing to replace a substandard Federal Pacific panel. The home inspector will call attention to a panel that is a fire hazard.

Is the main stack of the plumbing system corroded? That is a big red flag. Is there a puddle of water above the floor drain? What about leaks or water stains under sinks or leaky faucets or poor water flow coming out of the faucets? Take care of these items before listing the property or it will end up costing you more in the end. A licensed plumber can take care of these things in a couple of hours.

If the roof is old and the shingles are curling up at the edges, it makes sense to replace it. Most likely the age of the roof will be verified by the home inspection. A brand-new roof is a plus for buyers because it is considered a big-ticket item.

In Chapter 7 I will cover simple things that can be done to increase the value of a property without spending a lot of money. First impressions are essential, and the look of the exterior will determine whether a potential buyer will call their Realtor or keep on driving.

4. You may encounter unanticipated expenses. It makes sense to spend $100 or $200 for a sewer inspection because re-

placing a sewer line can cost thousands of dollars. You also need to budget for the cost of materials, contractor delays, holding expenses such as interest, utilities, taxes, and even the possibility that depending on the buyer, you may have to pay for closing costs.

5. You could lose money if you make poor decisions. However, a bad outcome is unlikely if you follow these five rules:

    - Fall in love with the deal and not the property.
    - Work with a Realtor who has personal experience flipping houses and can help you avoid making costly mistakes.
    - Know the cost of materials and labor and allow an additional 10–15% for unexpected expenses.
    - Figure out how much profit is required to make this a worthwhile project. (Use the good, better, best spreadsheet described in Chapter 8.)
    - Do your due diligence and do not skimp on the quality of workmanship.

    I hire contractors to perform renovation work because I believe my time is better spent helping clients than installing drywall. (Actually, I have no interest in doing any of the work, period.) Perhaps you have the time and skill to do this kind of work yourself. The real question is how involved you want to be, especially if you have a full-time job. Keep in mind that the longer it takes to get the job done, the less money you are making (holding costs increase over time).

6. Some people will tell you that flipping is stressful. I have worked with hundreds of investors who flip houses, and I can honestly tell you that none of my clients have ever shown signs of stress.

Some will say that stress can be caused by not finding the right property. Is that stress or impatience? You can avoid this type of stress by being patient until you find the right property with your Realtor. Remember that the goal is to make money.

Some will say stress is caused by waiting for a buyer. Is that real stress or unrealistic expectations? I do not work with any clients who use a hard money lender, but I can see how someone who does this could get stressed out if the property does not sell within the desired time frame. Hard money lenders loan money based on collateral securing the loan, so they are less concerned about your ability to repay the loan than a financial institution would be. If you cannot repay the loan, hard money lenders could foreclose and get their money back by seizing the property and selling it. Generally, a hard money loan must be paid back within a very short period of time.

7. If you make poor decisions, you could have a bad outcome. The biggest example of this type of error is falling in love with the property instead of the deal and paying too much for it. In addition, I have seen people get into real financial trouble because they did not have an experienced Realtor on their side and spent too much on remodeling costs. Perhaps they went to a seminar and were given the wrong information, or maybe they decided to go it alone.

    Certain types of improvements can help you get the maximum return on your investment. For example, updating the kitchen and bathrooms will make you money. The type of updating depends on the property's price point, but in my experience you do not need custom cabinets, and the ones you can purchase at Lowe's, Menards, Home Depot, etc., work great. Working with an interior designer is likely to cut deeply into your profits.

Most often, poor decisions come from getting in over your head and trying to go it alone. You can avoid poor decisions by working with a qualified Realtor every step of the way (be sure to choose an agent who has experience flipping properties) and by paying attention to quality, inspecting the work performed by contractors, and making sure the proper permits are obtained. Before you list the property, get it pre-inspected so you will have another set of eyes going over the property. It is better to find out about a problem right away than to overlook it and end up getting blindsided later.

Again, if you listen to the pundits, they will discourage you. I do not think there is one disadvantage that would discourage me from doing this. It's important to go into flipping with a realistic yet positive outlook. Dwelling on everything that could possibly go wrong might cause you to overlook the positive outcomes of flipping, which include making money and learning from your mistakes.

In summary, flipping is a terrific way to make a living if you do the proper due diligence and ask yourself these two questions before you list a renovated property:

- Am I happy with the workmanship?
- Would I buy this property?

Will you be able to sleep at night if you covered up something that might cause a problem for a young couple that are excited to purchase their first home and barely had enough money for their down payment? Let your conscience be your guide.

CHAPTER 5
ADVANTAGES OF BUYING AND HOLDING

By now, I am sure you can tell that I am deeply passionate about real estate. It is all about the "Big Why" of investing: wealth building, retirement income, and financial freedom. Investing in real estate has provided my family and me with financial freedom beyond anything I had ever dreamed about. It has been an amazing ride for more than 45 years, and I cannot think of any other investment option that offers so much for hard-working people who want to achieve financial independence.

I do not own even one share of stocks because I believe that I can do a much better job of managing my money than a financial advisor could. I appreciate having control over my investments, and I prefer to invest in something that I can see, touch, and understand.

> Anyone contemplating starting a real estate investment business should utilize the services of a competent and knowledgeable accountant and/or attorney

When I ask my clients why they want to invest in real estate (their "Big Why"), I am looking for specific responses that will tell me that they get it. "Cash flow" is not enough. Often their Big Why involves retirement income, but there are additional reasons that make sense.

No other investment option offers as many benefits as real estate, including appreciation, principal reduction, rental income (cash flow), and tax benefits. Still, there are more important reasons why a real estate business is the ticket to wealth building, retirement income, and ultimately financial freedom. (For the purposes of this book, a *real estate investment* is defined as a non-owner-occupied residential property.)

When was the last time you considered where you are in your retirement planning? This probably does not apply to you, but many people spend more time planning their next vacation than their retirement.

Let's do a quick gut check. How would you answer the following questions?

- How comfortable are you with your current economic situation?
- Are you on track to accomplish your retirement objectives?
- How did you come out on your taxes last year? Did you get a refund or pay more than your fair share of taxes? What are you planning to do differently this year?
- Are you happy with the return from your current investments?
- Do you feel that you are in control of your financial future or leaving it up to someone else?
- How much longer do you plan on working? To age 65 or older? Will you have enough money to maintain your current lifestyle during retirement?
- Are you prepared for life after work?
- What would happen if you got sick, if your position was eliminated, if you got fired or could no longer earn a living in the workplace?
- What is your current financial situation?
- Are you saving enough money regularly?
- Do you have enough disposable income?
- Are you more in debt than you would like?
- Do you have a lot of credit card debt?
- Are you living from paycheck to paycheck?
- Do you know what your net worth is?

Your answers to these questions will reveal your *Big Why.*

ARE YOU ON TRACK FOR A COMFORTABLE RETIREMENT?

When you think about it, why do you save or invest in the first place? If you are still working, your goal might be to have enough retirement income to maintain your current lifestyle after leaving the work force.

How often do you think about whether you will have enough money to enjoy your retirement? Do you feel confident that you will be able to travel or do other things that are on your bucket list?

You are working hard right now so that someday your money will work hard for you. You are counting on your investments to provide enough income to support your needs and lifestyle.

How many people do you know for whom the opposite is true? They make a decent income and perhaps earn more than $100,000 per year but have no real savings or retirement plan and live from paycheck to paycheck. Retirement is just a dream for them. This scenario probably applies to many of your neighbors, family members, and friends.

Although recent economic fluctuations have raised awareness of the importance of retirement planning, millions of Americans still have a dismal outlook regarding their ability to retire.

Luckily, there is a path out of financial insecurity. Investing in real estate puts you in control of your retirement income. For some investors, it can change their retirement outlook from negative to positive. How does real estate fit into your financial future?

REAL ESTATE OUTPERFORMS MOST OTHER INVESTMENTS

Many people have not considered the possibility of investing in real estate. When they think of investments, the first things that come to mind are stocks, bonds, a 401k, mutual funds, and so on. The fact that you are reading this book tells me that you are open to the idea of investing in real estate.

For the purposes of this book, a real estate investment is defined as a property that generates income or is otherwise intended for investment purposes rather than as a primary residence. It is common for investors to own several rental properties, not including their primary residence. In addition to the "Big Why," it is so popular because of the amazing benefits it provides, such as cash flow, appreciation, principal reduction, and tax benefits, all made possible by the most powerful tool of all—leverage. The tax implications of property ownership and transfer for real estate investors are different from those for homeowners.

A real estate investment business is an asset class in which people invest their hard-earned money with the expectation that they will receive profits. These profits may include cash flow, principal reduction, appreciation, and tax benefits.

Historically, real estate has shown consistent value growth. This growth occurs even during periods when other investment choices are less productive.

You already know about the advantages and disadvantages of flipping. Let us review that in the short term, money can be made relatively quickly. I am aware that prices in your community may be higher, but as an example, in Omaha, Nebraska, you might pay $100,000 to purchase a home that needs work. Your total expenses for rehabbing, holding costs, commissions, and so on are $35,000. Four months later, you sell the home for $180,000, earning a profit of $55,000 (less the selling costs and taxes). How many people do you know who can make that kind of money in such a short time? Some people work for an entire year and earn less than $55,000. (Keep in mind that the profits from flipping will be treated as ordinary income for tax purposes, so check with your accountant to determine the amount you will owe in taxes.)

Real estate also works well as a long-term investment. When you buy a rental property, your tenant ultimately is the one who reduces your mortgage balance each month. Building equity is the name of the game, and increased net worth is the outcome.

Income-producing properties can serve different purposes for different investors. A prudent way to supplement retirement income might be to start acquiring rental properties long before age 65. For example, if one starts investing in their thirties, by time they are in their sixties they could accumulate several million dollars' worth of real estate, generating a six-figure income. When the mortgages are paid off, the investor can live off the residual income during retirement. If you postpone investing until retirement age comes around, it is too late.

> Ultimately, the tenant is the one who is creating the retirement income and financial freedom you deserve. Do not get hung up on whether you are paying 1/2% more or less interest on a loan.

For a different investor, a more aggressive plan might be a better choice. This type of person might want to acquire a sizable portfolio of properties that generate enough cash flow that he or she will not have to rely on income from the workplace—the American dream of entrepreneurship in action.

WHY SHOULD YOU BUY AND HOLD REAL ESTATE?

Here are just a few reasons why real estate is one of the best investments around: leverage, positive cash flow, wealth building, hedge against inflation, portfolio diversification, tax deductions, 1031 exchange, tax-free cash refinance, and being your own boss. Each of these benefits is described briefly below and covered in detail elsewhere in this book.

➤ *Leverage*

Leverage is the use of borrowed funds to finance and accumulate real estate. Leveraging lets the investor use other people's money (OPM) to acquire properties. This is one of the most powerful tools investors can utilize because it allows them to purchase and finance increasing numbers of properties. Through leverage, they can substantially increase their return on investment (ROI). Gaining access to OPM is easy if the investor has a solid financial statement and is creditworthy. (Chapter 1 can help you figure out whether you are creditworthy.)

Few investment options other than real estate allow a person to make money on borrowed money. Based on a typical down payment of 20% to 25%, the potential profit on real estate is considerably higher than the profit for a non-leveraged investment such as stocks or mutual funds.

To illustrate the power of leverage, let us consider two different real estate scenarios with different ROIs.

In Scenario 1, you put a 20% down payment on a $100,000 property. You are controlling an asset worth $100,000 by investing only $20,000. In other words, you are using other people's money to make the purchase. (*Note:* I am aware that the average price of a home in your community may be higher or lower than $100,000.)

If your property generates $13,200 in yearly income and requires $5,000 in expenses, you have $8,200 in net operating income (NOI). Your NOI must be high enough to cover debt service to the bank, which is the principal and interest (PI) on your mortgage. Let's say your annual PI is $5,000, leaving you with $3,200 as your cash flow before taxes. To determine your return on investment (ROI), divide $3,200 by the total amount of cash invested. Your $20,000 down payment plus closing costs of $2,000 equals a total investment of $22,000. Divide $3,200 by $22,000, and you have an ROI of 14.5%.

In Scenario 2, you pay $100,000 cash for the property. The $100,000 selling price plus $2,000 closing costs equals a total investment of $102,000. You are not making any mortgage payments in this scenario, so your ROI is $8,200 (NOI) / $102,000 (Total Investment) = 8.0%. See why I recommend using the power of leverage by making a down payment instead of paying cash for a property?

By contrast with both the above scenarios, let us say you decide to invest $20,000 in the stock market. If your stock goes up 5% annually, your stock investment's value increases by $1,000 per year. How much of that $1,000 are you able to spend without selling the stock? *None of it.*

Could you buy $100,000 worth of stocks with $20,000? Yes. Buying on margin involves borrowing money from a broker to purchase stock. Buying stock on margin is only profitable if your stocks go up enough to pay back the loan with interest.

What happens when someone loses money on margin? A loss of 50 percent or more from stocks bought on margin equates to a loss of 100 percent or more, plus interest and commissions. In that scenario, you lose all of your own money, plus interest and commissions.

➤ *Cash flow*

Real estate should be a cash-generating investment. Buying only for appreciation is a mistake. Fall in love with the deal and not the property. Appreciation is a bonus. When you rent a property to a qualified tenant (having done due diligence in tenant selection to minimize risk), the rent payments should more than cover the mortgage payments, taxes, insurance, and maintenance. After these expenses are paid, the investment provides cash flow or residual income before taxes. When the property is paid in full, it is an excellent source of retirement income. How many people do you know who make $200 to $600 or more in monthly dividends (after all expenses) from investments other than real estate and can spend the money without being taxed? With stocks, you can either reinvest the dividends or cash out and pay taxes on your profits.

➤ *Wealth building*

Historically real estate has increased in value and should continue to do so over time. In other chapters, we will cover what classifies a property as a good investment that will build wealth over time, how and where to find such properties, and how to fund an investment property.

A real estate investment can build wealth in the following ways:

- *Appreciation*: Real estate tends to go up and down in value, but the long-term trend is upward. Why? The answer involves supply and demand. As Mark Twain said, "Buy land—they're not making it anymore." If the United States population continues to rise, good rental properties will always be in demand. And rents will tend to go up as well, especially if the property is well maintained and located in a desirable area. But keep in mind that the property must be maintained.

- *Tax benefits*: Deductions should offset the investor's tax liability for income from other sources (salary and other investments). (Note: Anyone contemplating the purchase of real estate should consult a competent legal professional and tax advisor.)
- *Principal reduction*: As you make payments on a mortgage each month, the amount you owe decreases slightly until the last payment is made and the loan is paid in full. This, too, is essentially paid by the tenant.

➤ *A hedge against inflation*

Real estate is one of the few assets that react proportionately to inflation. As inflation occurs, housing values increase and rents go up. Although some people see real estate as a risky investment, I believe real estate is one of the only safe investments left. Unlike the stock market, you cannot lose all of the money you have invested in a rental property. In addition, you can insure this asset.

➤ *Portfolio diversification*

As part of your investment portfolio, real estate allows you to avoid putting all your eggs in one basket. Most investment professionals agree that diversification will help you reach your long-range financial goals while minimizing risk. The key to successful diversification is finding a happy medium between risk and return.

Investments in each of the following asset categories do different things for you:

- Stocks help your portfolio grow.
- Bonds bring you income.
- Cash gives your portfolio security and stability.
- Real estate provides both a hedge against inflation and a low "correlation" to stocks—in other words, the value of your real estate may rise during periods when stock values fall.

➤ *Tax deductions*

When you or your accountant prepared your income tax returns last year, how happy were you with the amount of taxes you paid? More than likely, you felt that you paid too much tax because you did not have enough deductions. Most taxpayers probably feel the same way.

Do not get me wrong—I think paying taxes is a good thing because it means I am making money. But I believe in paying no more than my fair share of taxes. After all, the amount of money we make is less significant than how much we get to keep.

One of the best things about being a real estate investor is the many federal income tax advantages that become available to you. The Internal Revenue Service treats rental properties as a business venture, and therefore expenses involved in being a landlord are tax-deductible.

When you purchase real estate, one of the significant benefits, as previously discussed, is depreciation: 27½ years for residential and 39 years for commercial properties. When you buy stocks, you only get a tax break if you lose money on your investment; otherwise Uncle Sam gets his cut in the form of taxes.

➤ *1031 tax-deferred exchange*

Like-kind exchanges—when you exchange real property used for business or held as an investment solely for other business or investment property that is the same type or "like-kind"—have long been permitted under the Internal Revenue Code. Generally, if you make a like-kind exchange, you are not required to recognize a gain or loss under Internal Revenue Code Section 1031. If you also receive other (not like-kind) property or money as part of the exchange, you must recognize a gain to the extent of the other property and money received.

Properties are of like kind if they are of the same nature or character, even if they differ in grade or quality. Real properties generally are of like kind, regardless of whether they are improved or unimproved. For example, an apartment building would generally be like-kind to another apartment building or any type of real estate. However, real property in the United States is not like-kind to real property outside the United States.

(Source: Internal Revenue Service)

Example

> To defer 100% of the tax on the gain of the sale of the old property, the new property must be of equal or greater value. There are two requirements within this rule. First, the new property must be of greater or equal value than the one sold. Secondly, all the cash profits must be reinvested. You may deduct closing expenses and commissions from the sale of the property being sold. If the property is being sold for $400,000 and the actual net amount after closing expenses is $365,000, all that is required to be spent for the replacement property is a total of $365,000. Closing expenses associated with the purchase may be added into the purchase and capital improvements completed within 180 days together with furnishings.

> A party who elects to do an exchange and take cash out may do so. However, any cash received will be taxed at the corresponding rate of ordinary income if held for less than one year or 15% if held for more than one year. Anyone contemplating doing a 1031 exchange should verify the information. It is included here for illustrative purposes only, and they should seek the advice of a qualified tax advisor.

> *Refinancing*

As rents and property values go up, refinancing can be used to purchase additional properties. For example, let's say a property appraises for $100,000 and has a mortgage balance of $40,000. With a loan-to-value (LTV) ratio of 80%, the amount that you can pull out by refinancing your mortgage is $40,000 less refinance expenses.

Is it better to pay off the loan or refinance? The answer depends on your age, financial goals, and other factors.

> *Being your own boss*

One of the most powerful advantages of owning real estate is that you become your own boss. As a real estate investor, you get to choose which properties you will invest in, which tenants you will rent to, how much rent you will charge, and how you will manage and maintain the property. This is quite different from working at a job where you must do what your supervisor tells you to do. And when you work hard at a job, you are making the owner of the company wealthier, not increasing your own net worth.

Many people buy stocks in companies or shares in mutual funds without understanding why their investment value goes up or down. Who knows what the CEO or other people in the company are doing with your money? When you invest in stocks, there is nothing you can do personally to increase their value. But as a real estate investor you are in control, and the entire responsibility for the success or failure of your investment rests with you.

Real estate is a tangible asset. You can see it, drive by it, and improve it. You get to decide what to do or not do with it, and you will reap the benefits and pay the costs of your decisions.

DO YOU QUALIFY AS A "REAL ESTATE PROFESSIONAL" PER THE IRS? (AND WHY SHOULD YOU CARE?)

Individual investors like you and your neighbor account for almost 75% of rental properties in the United States, according to the U.S. Census Bureau's 2015 Rental Housing Finance Survey. How do we determine who is a "professional" in the real estate world, and more importantly, why do we care?

Real estate has countless tax advantages that often start to build up tax losses, and for someone who does not qualify as a real estate professional, these tax losses are deemed to be passive losses. A taxpayer may offset losses from a passive activity against income from a passive activity. A passive activity generally includes any trade or business of a taxpayer. The taxpayer does not materially participate and any taxpayer rental activities, regardless of the level of participation. However, if you qualify as an active investor and have less than $150,000 of adjusted gross income, you can deduct up to $25,000 of real estate losses.

As a qualified real estate professional, the rental activity is not presumed to be passive and will be treated as nonpassive if the taxpayer materially participates in the activity. This means that these real estate losses will allow the losses to be offset without limitation from any other income which you may have.

Passive investor: This is the least beneficial category and only allows passive losses with real estate, as mentioned above, to offset passive gains. This designation means that you are not actively involved in real estate investing. Typically, this designation means that you have put capital into a deal. However, someone else is managing everything, and you receive a return on your investment.

Active investor: This designation allows us to deduct up to $25,000 of losses against ordinary income. However, it is phased out entirely at $150,000 of adjusted gross income a year for a married couple filing jointly, or $100,000 for an individual. This is a designation when you actively are managing the property and involved. However, you do not qualify as a real estate professional.

Real estate professional: 100% of all real estate losses are deductible here against ordinary income. A taxpayer qualifies as a real estate professional if:

(a) The taxpayer spends more than one-half of the services the taxpayer performs in trades or businesses during the tax year in real property trades or businesses in which the taxpayer materially participates, and

(b) The taxpayer spends 750 hours or more (per year) in the real property business and rentals in which he or she materially participates.

Which category do you fall into? Are you taking advantage of all the possible tax benefits of your real estate holdings? If you need clarification, you should seek the advice of a qualified tax accountant.

HOW DOES REAL ESTATE COMPARE WITH STOCKS AND OTHER INVESTMENTS?

Each year Gallup asks Americans the following question: "Which of the following do you think is the best long-term investment: bonds, real estate, savings accounts or CDs, stocks or mutual funds, or gold?" For seven years in a row, real estate has come out on top as the best long-term investment.

In 2020 real estate was the top choice (35%), followed by stocks/mutual funds (21%), gold (16%), savings accounts/CDs (17%), bonds (5%), and others (6%).

Real estate is the top-ranking investment among most sub-groups of Americans across gender, age, and income categories—with a few exceptions. Young adults and residents of the East and Midwest are about equally likely to name stocks as real estate, and lower-income Americans' top choice is a tie between real estate and gold. The percentage who rank stocks as the best investment varies with household income, ranging from 19% among those earning less than $35,000 annually to 33% among those earning $75,000 or more.

Liquidity is commonly offered as proof that stocks are a better investment than real estate. I have sold houses that closed in one week. Even if it had taken two to three weeks to close the sale, as long as the profit was significant I would have been okay with the wait. With stocks, you can receive your money in two to four days. This comparison does not convince me that stock is a better investment than real estate.

It is my opinion (and you may not agree with me on this) that real estate is a far better investment than stocks, especially for the average hard-working American who has about $20,000 to invest. When the property is paid off, not only have you been receiving rent every month (which should include positive cash flow), but you own an asset that likely is worth a lot more than you originally paid for it.

Of all the investments within reach of the average individual, no other investment offers the full range of benefits available to real estate investors. Assets such as stocks, bonds, savings accounts, mutual funds, and CDs have pros and cons regarding "risk versus return." For comparison purposes, let us look at one more scenario that illustrates why investing in real estate is much better for most people than investing in stocks.

Let's say you have $50,000 to invest in either stocks or real estate. You could buy $50,000 worth of stocks or use the same amount of money to make a 20% down payment on real estate that has a total value of $250,000. Depending on your area, you might be able to purchase several properties that generate income. Keep in mind that investors generally buy properties that are good deals (priced 20% to 40% below what they sold for a few years ago). If you can find some good deals, your initial $50,000 could be controlling much more than $250,000 because the properties are worth more than their purchase price.

If the value of your stocks or real estate went up by, say, 10%, then your stocks would be worth $55,000, giving you a $5,000 profit. But your real estate would be worth $275,000, giving you $25,000 profit. That is a 50% return on your initial investment of $50,000.

How much control do you have over the future value of your $50,000 worth of stock? None. By contrast, could you do anything that might increase the value of your $250,000 worth of property? Since your properties are undervalued, they may need a little cosmetic work, such as paint, landscaping, new bathroom fixtures, or updated kitchen appliances. There are lots of things you can do to improve the property without spending a lot of money.

Now let's assume your stock does well and the shares you purchased double in value. Your $50,000 in stock is now worth $100,000. What can you do with the equity? Just one thing: sell your stock. Of course, that will create capital gains tax liability and reduce the amount you can invest now or in the future.

By contrast, let's say a few years go by, and your $250,000 property is now worth $500,000. What can you do to take advantage of the equity? You could sell the property, but that may not be the smartest option. Keep in mind the benefits your rental property provides in the form of cash flow, appreciation, tax advantages, and principal reduction, to name a few. Why would anyone want to sell a property that is increasing in value and generating income at the same time? What is more, if you did sell it, you would have to pay capital gains tax on the profit.

A better way to take advantage of the equity would be to re-finance the property or do a 1031 tax-deferred exchange. The money would not be taxable if you used it to purchase additional investment properties.

Or how about this scenario: Let's say you go back to your bank and ask for an 80% loan-to-value mortgage of $400,000. After paying off your original $200,000 loan, you would still have $200,000 that could be used as down payments (at 20% of the purchase price) to purchase more properties. That amount would give you $1,000,000 in purchasing power. The property you bought initially is now worth $500,000, and you have ac-quired additional property worth $1,000,000 for a combined real estate portfolio of $1,500,000.

This is the power of leverage hard at work. Equally as im-portant, the amount of principal reduction was not considered to simplify this explanation, but it would have made the scenario even better. Can you now see the power of investing in real estate compared to stocks?

Real estate is head and shoulders above any other investment. Imagine giving your stockbroker the following instructions:

"I would like to buy some stock, but I can only pay 20% down. I would like the stock to go up in value over time and pay dividends. When the stock goes up, I may want to pull tax-free cash out of it and keep the stock. At some point, I may also want to sell it and pay no taxes and then buy other stocks with the profit from the sale. Oh, and by the way, I would also like a tax deduction every year as long as I own this stock for the next 27½ years." (*Note:* A residential property can be depreciated for tax purposes for 27½ years and commercial property for 39 years.)

What do you think your broker's reaction would be? He or she would probably laugh out loud, thinking you were making a joke.

During the 45-plus years that I have been investing in real estate, I have enjoyed having a high level of control over my investments. I can take steps to improve my property and increase the income it generates. By contrast, I lost most of the money I invested in the stock market because I did not understand it and had to rely on my broker for advice. I even had to pay a commission to sell the stuff. But with real estate, my investment will always be worth something.

Do you know anyone who makes at least $200 per month in dividends that they can actually spend from investments other than real estate, with as little as $5,000, $10,000, or $20,000 invested in the stock? As a real estate investor, you can do this with just one rental (cash flow) while your tenants pay down your debt. I have personally witnessed many people become millionaires with this type of business. If you choose properties wisely and follow the advice in this book, you can build a sizable portfolio that generates a six-figure annual income with a small amount of effort.

> Some people confuse creating wealth with earning a high income. Do you know anyone who is making an excellent income at the workplace but living from paycheck to paycheck and not creating retirement income?

YOUR "BIG WHY" FOR REAL ESTATE INVESTING

As I emphasize throughout this book, your "Big Why" for real estate investing should always be to build wealth, earn retirement income, and/or achieve the financial freedom. If you are not on track to accomplish your retirement objectives, what are you planning to do differently? Keep in mind that the choices you make will either bring you closer to your goals or put you farther away from achieving the financial freedom you deserve.

I am confident that if you choose your properties carefully and intelligently, real estate investing can yield substantial benefits that cannot be achieved through any other investment type. Ultimately, attaining financial freedom is a very realistic goal.

Do not listen to the pundits. Real estate is the real deal. Andrew Carnegie once said that 90% of the world's millionaires got their wealth by investing in real estate. I say, "Buy today and profit tomorrow."

I have an excellent track record as an investor and have made a lot of money during my 45-plus years in real estate. And for more than 20 years as a Realtor, I have chosen to specialize in the investment "niche market." My greatest reward has come from helping many of my clients to become millionaire real estate investors.

I have seen too many colleagues and investors who made costly mistakes because they did not know what financial terms meant or why it is essential to run the numbers. Yes, analyzing a property is the most critical step.

Unfortunately, too many people fall in love with the property instead of the deal. They buy a property on emotion even though it may be a bad investment. If you do not run the numbers, how will you know if it is a great deal, a so-so deal, or a dud?

You see, I consider real estate a business, no matter whether you own one property or a hundred. Like any other enterprise, you have to make sure it will be profitable. Can you imagine, for example, starting a restaurant, body shop, or any other business without projecting your income and expenses?

I cannot think of any other business that is as terrific as real estate. Once the properties are paid off, they are the gifts that keep on giving and giving.

Real estate investments require some math because the last thing you want to do is leave things up to chance. Savvy investors learn these formulas inside and out so that they will be able to evaluate a potential investment in just a few minutes. For the most part, these formulas can be used to analyze any real estate options. I use them mainly with residential investments.

No matter whether you are a new investor or one with years of experience, these formulas will help you analyze properties so you can make good decisions. Ultimately, it comes down to either moving forward with a deal or walking away.

Purchasing a personal residence is different from buying an investment property, and emotion should not be part of the decision process for an investor. It comes down to "Will this property make me money? Will it be profitable?"

In the "Resources" section you will find a case study with 19 different formulas you can use to analyze a property under consideration and see if it will pass the test. Just knowing how to use four of these formulas—Net Operating Income, Cash Flow Before and After Taxes, Cash on Cash, and Cap Rate—will go a long way.

CHAPTER 6
DISADVANTAGES OF BUYING AND HOLDING

I will start this chapter by saying that if you are creditworthy and have the right reasons for investing in real estate (the "Big Why"), I personally think there are no real disadvantages of buying and holding residential properties compared with other types of investments. In my experience, the advantages far outweigh the disadvantages and most of the so-called disadvantages can be turned into advantages.

Jerry Sicuinas, the real estate agent who helped me get started, used to tell me, "You will never go wrong by investing in real estate. Others might try to talk you out of it, but it is your money and not theirs."

I will give you my take on some of the so-called disadvantages, but keep in mind that every business has drawbacks if you look for them. There are pros and cons to everything in life. If you allow others to discourage you from doing things, you will never get to where you want to end up.

I will make a bold statement: I believe the so-called disadvantages are nothing more than distractions raised by people who failed in this industry. Maybe they failed because they made emotional decisions or had a poor (or nonexistent) business model. I would not be where I am today if I had spent time dwelling on the potential disadvantages of this business. I had enough confidence to get started, and I hope you will, too.

1. One disadvantage that is sometimes mentioned is the fact that the closing costs of buying rental property are much higher than the transaction fees for purchasing shares of stock. However, the benefits also are much greater for real estate investors than for those who put their money in the stock market.

Here's an illustration. Let's say an investor buys $20,000 worth of stocks and pays $10 in transaction fees for a total investment of $20,010. How long will it take for the value of the stock to reach $100,000? Nobody knows. And how much will the investor earn in dividends per month that they can spend without paying taxes? None, because often dividends are distributed only when stock is sold, and profits from stock are treated as taxable income.

Now let us say that a savvy investor uses the same $20,000 as a down payment on a $100,000 property and pays closing costs of $1,000. In this scenario the total investment is $21,000.

The property generates cash flow of $300 per month, which means it will take roughly three months to pay off the closing costs. In addition, the principal owed on the mortgage will go down by a few hundred dollars during the same time period. Real estate, unlike stock, also provides benefits such as appreciation, tax breaks, and the power of leverage.

2. Another disadvantage mentioned by critics of real estate investment is that it takes a significant portion of the average American's net worth to fully own a rental property.

    Net worth is assets minus liabilities. What is your net worth, and how does it compare with that of other people in your age bracket?

    According to the latest Survey of Consumer Finances (conducted by the Federal Reserve every three years), the net worth of various age groups in the United States is as follows:

Individuals in their 20s:

- Average net worth: $56,984
- Median net worth: $6,500

Individuals in their 30s:

- Average net worth: $174,002
- Median net worth: $32,600

Individuals in their 40s:

- Average net worth: $457,783
- Median net worth: $93,460

Individuals in their 50s:

- Average net worth: $998,416
- Median net worth: $152,400

Individuals in their 60s:

- Average net worth: $1,121,534
- Median net worth: $221,200

If you use your own money to purchase a property and have no intention of refinancing, I would agree that you are at a disadvantage because you're not using the power of leverage. For the investors I work with, however, the following scenario is more typical.

1.) Buy a property for $80,000 using a line of credit (LOC).

2.) Do minor TLC that costs $10,000 using the LOC, for a total investment of $90,000.

3.) The appraised value of your property is now $120,000, which means you have equity of $30,000.

4.) Borrow $90,000 based on the appraised value of the house: $90,000 / $120,000 = 75% Loan to Value. Your bank is thrilled because they generally like an 80% loan-to-value ratio or less.

5.) You use the money from refinancing to pay off
the line of credit.

6.) You now control a property with $0 out of pock-
et and $30,000 in equity.

7.) The loan is for $90,000 amortized over 20 years
at 4.5% interest. The principal and interest payments are
$569.38, taxes are $166.66, and insurance is $100, for a
total monthly payment of $869.38.

8.) The property rents for $1,250 per month

9.) $1,250 – $869.38 = $330.62 monthly cash flow.
$330.62 X 12 = $3,967.44 yearly income from this investment.

How many people do you know who are getting this kind
of return with none of their own money? It happens! I've seen it
work this way many, many times.

Have I debunked the idea that owning real estate is unrealistic for most people because it would take a significant portion
of the average American's net worth? How much of the investor's
own money was used in this example? Did it take a significant
portion of their net worth to fully own a rental?

How you invest your money is up to you, but if you are not
happy with the return from your current investments and you
prefer to take charge of your financial future, look no further
than real estate. You will be glad you did!

3. Another so-called disadvantage of owning a rental property is the fact that certain expenses are unavoidable, such as real estate taxes, insurance, and maintenance. And if you choose not to deal directly with tenants, you will need to hire a property manager.

    News flash: Expenses like these are the cost of doing business. They are not a disadvantage; they are a fact of life.

    > Always remember that a disadvantage can be turned into an advantage. Seeking advice from others is important, but at the end of the day, it is your money.

4. Liability is sometimes mentioned as a disadvantage of investing in real estate. Liability protection should not be taken lightly. It is critical to work with a competent attorney who can help you establish iron-clad protection measures, starting with a lease that outlines your responsibilities and those of your tenants. Another common protection measure involves establishing an LLC. Your attorney can help you decide whether or not to take this step.

    Umbrella insurance is an excellent investment for landlords. Such policies are relatively inexpensive and a highly effective way to reduce your liability.

5. Another "disadvantage" cited is that unexpected expenses may occur. Doing proper due diligence before the purchase will help you avoid unpleasant surprises. For example, obtaining a sewer inspection before purchasing a property can protect you from having to pay thousands of dollars to replace a worn-out sewer line.

6. Vacancies may occur from time to time in any rental property, and some people see this as a disadvantage. However, vacancies should be rare if the property is well maintained and located in a family-friendly neighborhood. In addition, your lease should require 60-days' notice before termination. During this two-month period, the property can be shown to prospective tenants.

7. Values of real estate can go up and down, and the potential for decreases in value is viewed as a disadvantage by some people. In my opinion, this situation is unlikely to occur if you follow rule #1: Fall in love with the deal and not the property. Buy undervalued properties so you can update them to increase their value and still have equity. If you do this, the value of the property is not going to decrease.

   And even if the value of the property does go down, you will still be okay. Here's an illustration: You buy a house for $100,000, and 15 years from now it appraises at $90,000. Are you worse off than you were when you bought the house? No. The property has been rented for the past 15 years, so your tenants have paid off the mortgage and created wealth for you.

8. Some people will tell you that lack of liquidity is a disadvantage of investing in real estate, but I disagree. I have bought and sold properties in less than one week. If you sell your shares of stock, it takes 3 to 4 days to receive your money. Even if one must wait a few days longer to get a nice check from the sale of your flip or long-term rental, this should not hold you back from investing in real estate. If you have an emergency and need money immediately, you can always use a line of credit to borrow the money. If you pay off the line of credit as soon as possible, the interest will be insignificant.

9. The tenant may damage the property. Unfortunately, this may happen from time to time. However, over the years that I have been doing this, the percentage of significant damage caused by tenants is exceptionally low. Some believe this risk is worse than it actually is.

   Obtaining before-and-after pictures and/or videos will make it difficult for the tenant to prove that they did not cause the damages. Even before the lease is signed, carefully go through the unit with the tenant and document any damages.

   Yes, damages will occur, but they can be minimized. I always followed a simple rule: own properties in family-friendly neighborhoods that attract quality tenants who will take care of the property.

   If the tenant causes damages that are not considered normal wear and tear, you can deduct the cost of repairs from the security deposit. If damages exceed the deposit and the tenant refuses to pay you the difference, you can sue the tenant in small claims court.

10. Some may see not being handy as a disadvantage and a reason not to invest in real estate, but I see it as an excuse. They are missing the big picture of wealth creation. Not being handy is not a justifiable reason to avoid investing in real estate.

11. Some people will say they do not have enough time to manage properties. The real question to ask is why they don't have the time. Is it because they are spending two-thirds of their life working for someone else and helping that person create wealth, or is it because they would rather play golf three times a week? There are 24 hours in the day, and there is plenty of time to do whatever we decide is important.

Wealth building, retirement income, and financial freedom are well worth the time and effort involved. Your sacrifices will be rewarded when you need it most—at retirement.

Instead of spending my time working for somebody else or playing golf, I prefer to be in charge of my financial future by investing in real estate. I can play as much of an active role as possible or hire a property manager to handle the day-to-day functions of the business.

Always remember that wealth is found on the other side of fear. Doing the proper due diligence and having the right team on your side (a qualified Realtor, attorney, accountant, property manager, insurance agent, contractors, and so on) will go a long way toward making sure your assets are well-protected. Do not try to do everything by yourself. In particular, a Realtor who has expertise and experience in residential property investments will be your greatest asset.

If you're still not sure about investing in real estate, think about the people who started a business and had to close their doors due to a lack of cash flow. Did you know that 82% of businesses close for that reason? By contrast, cash flow is one of the benefits of investing in real estate.

Real estate was put to the test during COVID-19 and survived. Some landlords took a temporary hit due to the moratorium on evictions, but it ended before you started reading this book.

Again, real estate has met the test of time. It is the best business to own because housing will always be a necessity.

CHAPTER 7
THE FABFS/R SYSTEM:
FIND, ANALYZE, BUY, FIX, SELL/RENT

Have you decided whether you want to flip properties, buy and hold, or do some of each? No matter which path you take, the five-step system described in this chapter will work for you.

At this point, the second-biggest mistake you can make is to think you can just fly by the seat of your pants. What is the biggest mistake? Never getting started due to fear of the unknown. Money is on the other side of fear!

Hundreds of books have been written about investing in real estate, and I have read some of them; however, most of my knowledge comes from practical experience. Like many others, I made a lot of mistakes early in my venture. I learned through trial and error—buying the wrong properties in areas I should have avoided, paying too much for properties, overspending on renovations, and so on. Fortunately, real estate is very forgiving and I learned from my mistakes.

GET OFF THE STARTING BLOCK

Nothing will be lost if you do not take the next step, and nothing will be gained. If you choose to start investing in real estate, however, you will begin a new and exciting chapter in your life. You will be able to enjoy all the benefits that real estate offers, including tax deductions and additional income.

This chapter will take you step by step through the system I have used in my own real estate business and shared with my clients for many years. This system will give you a solid foundation for building wealth by investing in real estate.

If you find the right real estate agent and follow my model, you can avoid the trial-and-error stage and produce measurable and worthwhile results that can be repeated over and over.

THE SYSTEM

According to Business Dictionary.com, a system is "a set of detailed methods, procedures, and routines created to carry out a specific activity, perform a duty, or solve a problem."

To use my system effectively, you will need to develop clear guidelines for the properties you will consider, the properties you will buy, and the properties you will walk away from.

The types of properties that generally offer the best opportunity for immediate equity are foreclosures, REOs (properties owned by financial institutions), estate sales, properties that have been neglected and need cosmetic improvements, properties that have been tagged by the city for violations, and properties that have been listed for several months and are vacant. There are lots of other ways to purchase properties such as auctions, "for sale by owners," or wholesalers.

Regardless of how one acquires property, prices are going through the roof as I am writing this book in 2021. Foreclosures and short sales are pretty much nonexistent.

Keep in mind that location, location, location should always be considered when deciding whether to make an offer. Buying real estate in various locations is a lot like buying blue-chip versus penny stock. Your real estate agent should be aware of the emerging areas in your community and able to find available properties that you are likely to be interested in. Your goal is to purchase undervalued properties that have a big enough spread to achieve the desired profit.

Since investors come from all walks of life and have different reasons for investing, a one-size-fits-all strategy will not work. Factors to consider may include how much money you want to invest, your age, your needs, whether you are looking for short-term profit or long-term income, how much risk you are comfortable with, and so on. With your real estate agent's help, you will need to develop your own criteria for choosing properties.

If you have the correct mindset, if your agent finds deals for you and helps you analyze the property and negotiate the deal, and if the property gets to the closing table, you will see how powerful the relationship between you and your agent can be for many years to come. It is a WIN-WIN. Your agent helps you accomplish your objectives, and you help them make a good living.

A deal today is different from what a deal was like five to seven years ago; however, there's no bad time to get in the "game." As an example, in the metro Omaha area in 2009 the median sales price was $130,000. At the end of 2020 it was $218,700. What is the appreciation in your community?

My five-step system, F-A-B-F-S/R, is summarized below. Each step will be described in detail in this chapter.

Step 1. **FIND**

Select a property that has investment potential. If the property is truly a great deal, you must act quickly before it is gone. Keep in mind that you are competing with other investors for limited available properties. Does the property initially meet your objective of maximizing the profit, given the risks? If yes, move to the next step.

Step 2. **ANALYZE**

Depending on the type of property; this step may be extremely easy to accomplish. If it is a single-family dwelling, comparable properties are the best indicator of the value after fix-up costs. If it is a multi-unit, more information is required to run the numbers. If the property passes the analysis, move on to writing an offer. See the sample formulas that can help you determine whether it makes sense to have the agent write the offer or not. Remember the rule that says you should fall in love with the deal and not the property.

Step 3. BUY

Write the offer while paying attention to the bottom line. If your offer is accepted, follow through with the purchase and then go to the next step. Get the property under contract and do the necessary due diligence such as a home/investor inspection to find deficiencies. Remember that every imperfection is not a major problem. If it gets a passing grade, move forward and close on it. If not, walk away.

Step 4. FIX

Make repairs and updates to get optimum rents or profits. Staying on budget is critical.

Step 5. SELL / RENT

Flip quickly or rent the property after repairs have been made within the desired time frame and budget.

In the rest of this chapter, we will take a closer look at each of the five steps.

Step 1: Find a property

A key factor in finding an investment property is to base your decision on numbers rather than emotion. Keep in mind that this is a business venture, not playtime. As an investor, you should buy a property because it is a good deal, based solely on the numbers. Will the property meet your short- and long-term financial objectives? Simply put, that means looking at cash flow and tax benefits for a rental property. What if you are buying it to flip? To evaluate a potential flipper, answer the following questions:

1. What can the property sell for, based on prices of comparable properties in the same neighborhood?

2. How much will it cost to make the needed repairs and updates?

3. How much profit do you want to make?

If you pay too much for a property or spend too much improving it, the desired profit may not become a reality.

Your real estate agent should be able to recognize a good deal. They know and understand the local housing market, and their knowledge will bring tremendous value to you. Experienced real estate agents who are also investors bring a wealth of knowledge based on experience, research, and education.

Different ways to find a good deal

Good deals are not as readily available as they were a few years ago, but they still exist. Investors who utilize a knowledgeable real estate agent should expect their agent to spot the good deals that exist.

- *Multiple Listing Service (MLS)*

There are many ways to find properties for investment purposes, but my primary choice is MLS. Although the competition is fierce for properties with investment potential, your agent should be able to find properties that will meet your criteria. Sometimes searching the MLS four or five times a day instead of once a day makes a difference between finding properties and overlooking them.

Your agent may be on the lookout for expired listings, properties that have been listed for 90 days or more, and properties that have been reduced in price, are vacant, and so on. They can utilize search terms such as foreclosure, REO, cosmetics, estate motivated, must sell, as is, handyman, TLC, and cash only. Keep in mind that a suitable property for one investor may not be ideal for another. What criteria are important to you?

- *Networking and Word of Mouth*

If your real estate agent is a residential investment specialist, they are likely to network with other real estate agents who also work with investors (not just agents in their own company). When they are engaged in this niche market, they know other agents who are doing the same thing. This is not about competition but about helping sellers sell their property in the shortest amount of time.

How many real estate agents in your community specialize in investment properties? There are probably very few compared with the number of real estate agents who compete fiercely for residential owner-occupied listings and sales. Agents who specialize in investment properties may know agents who list foreclosures and short sales.

Your agent can let other agents know that they have buyers who are always looking for properties in need of repairs (cosmetic or major work). These properties make great flipping candidates or rentals. Perhaps these other agents have no interest in working with investors. This can be a highly effective strategy because other agents might not have a potential buyer for this type of property.

- *Advertise*

Some real estate agents may advertise in your local newspaper's real estate section that they have buyers who are looking for properties in any condition.

- *Visit the county assessor's website*

Some real estate agents obtain from the county assessor a list of all the multi-units in the community. Owners who have multiple properties or live out of state may have residential properties that they want to sell.

- *Websites*

An innovative way to buy real estate is through online auctions. However, there are often restrictions that could cause you to make a serious blunder. For example, you may be prohibited from going into the property. Inspections and due diligence are essential before making an offer. If you can't enter a property, how can you estimate how much renovation will be needed?

Here are several websites where you can search for properties not only in your community but throughout the United States.

- ▶ Craigslist.com. This free website has a Real Estate tab for property owners and real estate agents. This can be a good place to spot opportunities.
- ▶ Auction.com auctions all types of real estate, including foreclosures, REOs, short sales, notes, commercial real estate, luxury real estate, new construction, and land. These auctions take place online, locally on-site, or in courthouses, as well as in live mega-auctions in meeting halls.
- ▶ Realtor.com is the official site of the National Association of Realtors®. You can access millions of listings compiled from over 800 MLS databases throughout the country. You also have the option to search exclusively for foreclosures.

▶ Roofstock.com is designed exclusively for buying and selling rental properties. A unique aspect of Roofstock is that investors can buy properties sight unseen, thanks to the company's certification process and national network of experienced property managers and partners.

▶ PropStream.com is a cutting-edge site where professional real estate investors use data software and analytics to conduct real-world investment analysis in multiple ways.

▶ DealMachine.com has moved the process of driving for dollars into the 21st century by automating real estate prospecting. Instead of wasting valuable time and money, today's investor can conveniently prospect from the comfort of a home office.

▶ Zillow.com is a very user-friendly website. To find property, you type in your search criteria. Your search can be as simple or as in-depth as you wish. You can simply enter a location for a basic search or type in factors such as type of property, price, and foreclosure status to do a more specific search.

▶ RealtyTrac.com. This site focuses on foreclosures. You can search the latest foreclosure listings across the country as well as learn the basics of foreclosures. This site has ample information on everything from how to buy foreclosures to the latest news and statistics on foreclosures.

▶ *PropertyShark.com* focuses on providing property records. Property records are useful for evaluating investment property because they contain important information such as the owner's name and address, assessed taxes, square footage, and purchase price.

Why should you focus on finding good deals?

When you purchase an undervalued property, you gain instant appreciation. Keep in mind that if a property is ready to move into, an owner-occupied buyer will likely pay more than you would.

Whenever possible, you want to buy properties that could become more valuable with some type of improvement. Potential improvements are described later in this chapter.

Your real estate agent should understand why it is important for you to purchase properties that are good deals. There is no reason for you to chase properties that do not meet your criteria. There will be a property tomorrow that will be better suited for you.

I study the MLS regularly and look at the properties that sold, and it amazes me what people paid for some of the properties. I am thinking to myself, "Are they nuts? What is their experience level or that of their real estate agent?"

Do you know anyone who overpaid for a property? No amount of wishing or praying is going to make that investment worthwhile or profitable. Did they fall in love with the property instead of the deal?

What about someone who bought with the idea of yearly appreciation and then the market took a downturn and values dropped as in 2008? They end up owing more than the property is worth. An investor should buy a property based on how much it is worth right away (after fix-up has taken place), not what they hope it will be worth in the future.

Your defined criteria will keep you focused on buying only properties that meet your objectives. If you find a property that meets your criteria, do not get stuck in "analysis paralysis." Pull the trigger and have your agent write an offer.

Do not just tell your agent to find a deal for you; be more specific. What area(s) will you consider? How many bedrooms, baths, and garages? What is the desired price range? Do you want to look at properties that are ready to go or only properties that need work? Make sure you give your agent the specifics needed to guide their search.

Criteria may include any or all the following: price range, location, schools, amenities/features, property condition, construction (brick or frame), number of bedrooms and bathrooms, with or without garages, close to a college or medical school, style of home or property, a property that needs minimal work and is virtually ready to rent, a property that needs updating to flip, and so on. But ultimately, the property can be considered a good deal if it makes sense financially.

Based on the above, you now have enough information to establish a plan of attack. It is like digging for gold to find the types of properties you are likely to purchase.

Classifying properties as A, B, C, D

As you evaluate properties, it is essential to use a consistent system. For our purposes, we will classify properties as A, B, C, or D.

These letter grades are assigned to properties and areas based on characteristics such as age, property condition, growing or declining areas, appreciation potential, amenities, and possible rental rates, to name a few features.

It is essential for you to understand various property classes and areas so you know why a property in area D costs much less than a similar property in area B.

It is essential to recognize the values of similar properties in different areas and how these differences can affect your investment goals.

Characteristics of properties

Although assigning letter grades to properties can sometimes be more of an art than a science, the property classes will typically have the following characteristics:

1. "A" property

These types of properties are like blue-chip stock. They tend to be newer (built within the last fifteen years), have the most up-to-date amenities, and demand the highest rents. There is no deferred maintenance. Older properties in excellent condition in extremely desirable areas can also fall into this category, as can properties near universities.

2. "B" properties

These types of properties may be a notch or two below an A property. They may not have all the amenities. They tend to be a bit older and will not command as much rent. They may have some deferred maintenance. They usually have appreciation potential. The savvy investor can quickly raise the property's value by making minor improvements.

3. "C" properties

These types of properties are typically older properties (built 30+ years ago) with far fewer amenities. They may be a notch or two below a B. They may be in up-and-coming neighborhoods. Rents are lower than for B properties. They usually have more deferred maintenance. The savvy investor can very quickly transform a C into a B by making minor improvements.

4. "D" properties

These types of properties are located in undesirable areas such as high-crime neighborhoods. The neighborhood is a bigger problem than the property's condition, because properties can be improved but little can be done about the community.

D properties may have a lot of deferred maintenance. Rents are low, and the quality of the tenant may not be excellent. Unless the neighborhood turns around, there will probably be little to no appreciation. They require intense management. These types of properties are not recommended for the brand-new investor.

A lot of money is being made in this space, and although D properties are cash flow machines, they require a lot of attention and repairs. These properties can be compared to a penny stock: high risk, high reward. The more important issue is what kind of image you want to maintain in your community.

Characteristics of neighborhoods

Your real estate agent should be knowledgeable about areas that are improving and areas that are declining. Depending on the neighborhood, a D property today could become a B property in a few years and vice versa.

When you evaluate areas, you can use a similar A, B, C, D classification system:

A – Newer growth areas

B – Older areas that are stable

C – Older declining or stable areas

D – Areas that are older, declining, or potentially rapidly declining

These guidelines will help determine the property types and locations you are interested in. The key is to identify properties that will accomplish your investment goals.

In choosing a property, you should focus on properties in areas that are equal to or better than the class of the property itself (for example, a B property in a B or A area) and avoid properties in areas that are lower than the property class (for example, an A property in a C area). The area will have a great deal of influence on your portfolio's stability over time and will determine whether it appreciates or declines in value during periods of economic fluctuation. An A property will have a much harder time performing like an A property if it is in a C area, but a C property might perform better over time if it is in an A area.

Suppose you are looking for investments with the highest appreciation potential and the best initial cash flow. In that case, you may consider looking for A and B properties located in A and B areas or in the path of progress. You will want to avoid properties in C areas. If you are not as interested in appreciation but are looking for investments with strong cash flow, then B and C properties in B and C areas would be the best fit.

If you are looking for a lot of cash flow and do not care about anything else, a D property may be an excellent option.

Now that you are more familiar with the ABCs of property and location classifications and how they can affect the value of an investment, you will be better able to select properties that meet and exceed your investment goals.

Step 2: Analyze a property

The most important criterion for choosing a property is the financial component, and every offer you make should be based on careful analysis to maximize profits given the risks.

Depending on the type of property being evaluated, the analysis can be straightforward to do. If it is a single-family dwelling, comparable properties' selling prices are the best indicator of value after fix-up costs. Multi-unit properties are evaluated differently.

A house is quite simple to analyze. How much rent can you expect compared to the monthly PITI (Principal, Interest, Taxes, and Insurance)? If a three-bedroom property rents for $900 and the PITI is $600, the cash flow is $300 a month before expenses. Is this a worthwhile investment or not? The simple answer is yes. You also should consider the financial impact of repairs, vacancies, and possibly property management.

What if you are interested in buying a duplex or a fourplex? How would you determine whether it is a good deal? Running the numbers will tell you whether the subject property is a poor or good investment opportunity.

To recognize whether a property is likely to be a good investment, consider cash flow, leverage, equity, appreciation, and risk.

1. Cash Flow

- Will this property produce the desired cash flow?
- What is the current rental market like?
- What is the vacancy history for this property?
- How much is the down payment (10%, 20%, 30%, or more)?
- What is the interest rate?
- Will this property provide the desired income?
- How important is income now to you compared with accomplishing your wealth and retirement income objectives in 10 to 20 years?
- Do you have another source of income?
- Is future equity important to you?
- How will this property's cash flow compare with that of other properties you are considering?

You should look at all of these factors when you are evaluating a property. For example, if you are analyzing several properties in the same neighborhood, ask yourself whether a $50,000 house that rents for $750 a month would be a better deal than a $100,000 duplex that rents for $1,050 per month or a $150,000 fourplex that brings in $2,000 per month. Instead of buying a duplex for $100,000, would it make more sense to purchase two $50,000 houses to produce a combined rental income of $1,500 per month? Would the two homes cost more to maintain than the duplex would cost? If so, how much more? Which of these potential purchases would be a better investment?

There are no right or wrong answers to these questions, but cash flow should always be considered when looking at a potential purchase. Keep in mind that the above prices are for illustration purposes only, and you can determine the appropriate values for your community and decide what is best for you.

2. Leverage

The less cash you use as a down payment on each property, the more buying power you will have and the greater the opportunity to expand your portfolio.

The following example illustrates the benefits of leverage:

- Investor A purchases a property for $200,000 cash. The property appreciates 5% in the first year ($10,000), so the return on investment is 5%.
- Investor B purchases a property for $200,000 with a $20,000 down payment and a mortgage of $180,000. The property appreciates 5% in the first year ($10,000). Based on the initial $20,000 investment, the return on the investment is 50 percent. Investor B benefits significantly from the power of leverage.

3. Equity

There are many ways to create equity, but the easiest way is to buy a property that is a great deal. All of the following types of properties could be great deals:

- An undervalued property
- A potential fixer-upper
- A rezoning opportunity
- A poorly managed property
- A foreclosure
- A short sale

4. Appreciation

If a property is a great deal, appreciation and equity will happen instantly. Buying in the right neighborhood should minimize your risk. In today's market, an investor should be able to purchase a property at 20% to 40% below or above the price that the same property sold for a few years ago.

5. Risk

- How much risk are you willing to take?
- What happens if your assumptions are not correct?
- Can you continue making the mortgage payment if you have a vacancy?

If you have done your due diligence and are comfortable with the level of risk involved in a potential purchase, you are well on your way to succeeding in this business.

How to gather property information

Before you make an offer, it is essential to know what factors contribute to a property's value.

Accurate information is critical. The minimum information needed before you can make an informed decision to either buy or pass on a property may include property details, financing, income generation, and expenses.

Property details. How old is the house or building (new, old, or run-down)? How many units does it have? Does the owner pay for the utilities, or are the units separately metered? How much does the property cost? What are the expected costs for any repairs or updates?

Financing details. What is the loan amount, down payment, closing cost, loan terms (10, 20, 25, 30 years), and interest rate?

Potential income. How much revenue does the property generate (rent, laundry machines, vending machines, and so on)?

Expenses. What is the annual cost to operate the property? Include such things as taxes, insurance, maintenance, lawn care, snow removal, advertising, supplies, and so on. Also, consider setting aside funds to cover the cost of deferred maintenance. A good property inspector can point out significant repairs or expenses that the property is likely to incur in the future (for example, replacing the roof, furnace, central air units, and so on).

The income minus expenses determines the net operating income (NOI). NOI is one of the most important measures used to determine a property's income stream.

All of the information you are working with must be accurate to determine whether a property is a great deal, an okay deal, or a horrible deal. The property's value is related to how much income/profit the property produces for the investor.

It is not uncommon for a seller to provide inaccurate numbers. For example, they may inflate how much rent the property produces, not include any vacancies, and overlook certain maintenance expenses. In other words, by overestimating income and underestimating costs, they make the property seem to be more valuable than it actually is.

Your agent will be critically important in helping you make the right decision. Make sure you have the best available information, all or most of which can be verified. (You may ask for tax returns for the past two years, for example.)

If the seller uses a property management company, they should be able to give you accurate information.

Are you familiar with the difference between *pro forma* information and information?

Pro forma means "estimated," and that is the information that is generally found on the MLS listing. You can analyze a property using pro forma, but it is better to base your analysis on actual details. Ideally, the pro forma will match the actual information.

Another piece of information to consider is the assessed value of the property. Are the taxes going up or down? It will make a difference on the bottom line if the income goes up and the expenses go down or vice versa.

It may not be a good idea to spend a lot of time analyzing before a property is under contract. Depending on your experience and the property's complexity, a detailed analysis can also be done in at the next stage.

Step 3: Buy the right property, based on your needs and objectives

Everything that needs to happen from purchase agreement to closing occurs at this stage. It is also essential to do whatever due diligence is desired: inspections by contractor(s) to determine whether the expected remodeling costs are satisfactory. Of course, "satisfactory" will have a different meaning for each investor. One of the most critical inspections to do is a sewer line inspection (using a camera). You will be able to know if the sewer line has shifted, is cracked, or is full of roots. If you skip this step, you could end up paying thousands of dollars to replace the sewer line.

What if the property is a multi-unit? The same due diligence may apply, but the decision to buy is also subject to insurance quote or inspection of all units, review, and approval of leases, tax returns, rent rolls, and so on. The greater the amount of due diligence that can be accomplished at the analysis stage (step 2), the better. However, sellers are sometimes reluctant to provide information until the property is under contract.

If the property meets the criteria, the offer is either written or not written at this stage. If a property will be used as a rental, the investor may be able to pay more than if it is intended as a "flipper."

CASH FLOW GROWTH

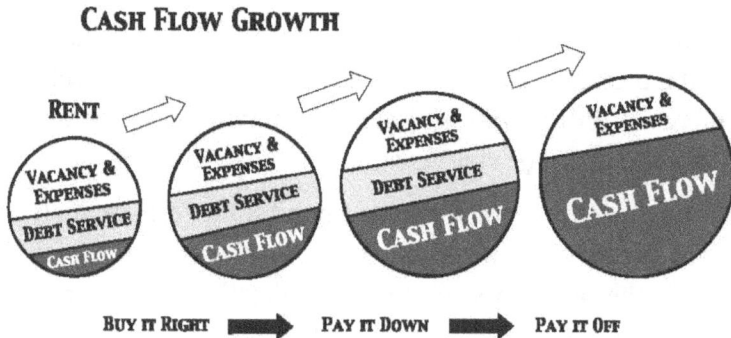

BUY IT RIGHT ➡ PAY IT DOWN ➡ PAY IT OFF

For a rental, the bottom line is how much income the property will produce. Over the long term, paying $5,000 to $10,000 more for a property may not make much of a difference in the monthly payment (PITI). An additional $5,000 at 5% interest with 20% down amortized over 20 years will be an extra $33 dollars a month in the payment. Sometimes buyers lose sight of the big picture and fail to realize that it might make sense to pay a little more for a property that will generate more income.

For a property purchased to flip, a higher price may not be feasible. A price that is $5,000 to $10,000 higher than your desired price may interfere with your ability to pay for a big chunk of the remodeling expenses.

How will the offer be written?

Will the offer be written as cash or conventional financing? Keep in mind that the preferred method of acquiring these types of properties is cash. This does not mean that an offer subject to a loan cannot compete with one from a cash buyer, but there is a good chance that even if the cash offer is lower, it will get the nod. Sellers prefer cash offers because there is no need for appraisals to meet underwriting guidelines.

Other options for making cash offers include a line of credit or bridge loan if the subject property is not used as collateral. The collateral may be the buyer's personal residence, securities, or other assets. The buyer may be able to use this method to purchase and fix a property and then have it reappraised and perhaps pull all their money back in. Your experience level, creditworthiness, financial statement, and so on will affect the feasibility of this approach.\A little-known fact is that investors can use their self-directed/Roth IRAs to purchase properties. A self-directed IRA requires account owners to make active investments on behalf of the plan. To open this type of account, an owner must hire a trustee or custodian to hold the IRA assets and be responsible for administering the account and filing required documents with the IRS.

Lately, many real estate agents and investors have been getting frustrated because they cannot find "deals." The common complaint is that when a property that is priced right hits the market, multiple offers lead to a bidding war that raises the actual selling price. This is different from the real estate market a few years ago when investors enjoyed the best opportunities in over 40 years.

I am not saying that good deals are not available. It is all relative. Even if you pay more for a property, keep in mind that rents also are going up and so are the selling prices of flipped properties. The bottom line is that "lowball" offers are more likely than ever before to be a waste of time.

After you have purchased an investment property, the next step is to improve it.

Step 4: Fix the property

This is the stage when you will make repairs and/or updates to get optimum rents or profits. Staying on budget with the remodeling project is crucial.

How will you know whether certain repairs should be made? To illustrate how to make this decision, let us use an example of a $60,000 property that requires $15,000 in repairs for a total investment of $75,000.

Scenario 1

Let us say that comparable properties in the same neighborhood sell in the $110,000 range and the investor bought the property intending to flip it. Carrying costs and selling expenses are $12,000, for a total expenditure of $87,000. The spread is a potential profit of $23,000 with fewer tax consequences. Not a bad return in just a few short months. The credit line is paid back, and the investor moves on to the next deal.

Scenario 2

If the property is going to be used as a rental, it must be nice enough to attract desirable tenants.

Rental properties are intended to be workhorses and not racehorses. They should be upgraded to a level that sets the tone for how the tenant should treat the property. First impressions are essential, and tenants should be just as picky about the property as the investor should be about the tenant. I believe that when tenants know what is expected, they will meet those expectations.

The more time you spend upfront fixing up the property, the more pride the tenant will have. When tenants see the owner taking an interest in the property, they will be more inclined to take care of it. A property that is in disrepair sends a strong message that the landlord only cares about collecting the rent.

If a property is in poor condition, the tenants are not likely to be "blue ribbon." On the opposite side, well-maintained properties attract tenants that are likely to do their part to maintain the property.

Every two to three months, take the time to check the condition of your investment. Be sure to give the tenants at least 24 hours' notice before entering the property. Driving by the property is also a good idea. Your inspection will give you a lot of clues on how well the tenants are taking care of your investment. Keep in mind that your rental property represents a lot more than just cash flow. It is your wealth and retirement.

Cosmetic versus structural problems

It may seem like an easy task to determine whether an issue with a property is a minor or significant problem, but it depends on the person who is doing the evaluating.

From a seller's perspective, all the issues with their property are minor problems. Many problems may be considered minor because they are common to a specific type of property of a given age and price range.

From a buyer's perspective, some problems are major, some are minor, and many are between the two. A home inspector or contractor can help you distinguish between minor and major problems.

Opportunities to purchase properties with minor or major issues can be found quite readily on the MLS. For the savvy investor, dollar signs are written all over them.

The lists that follow should make it easier to distinguish between cosmetic issues and significant problems.

Cosmetic issues

- Peeling interior/exterior paint
- Worn-out carpet
- Scratched or worn-out wood floors
- Old light fixtures
- Damaged kitchen cabinets
- Old or outdated ceramic/vinyl floor
- Junk and debris on a property sold "as is"
- Overgrown lawn
- Property tagged by code inspector (the violation may be major or minor)
- Worn-out siding
- Old appliances
- Outdated bathrooms/kitchen
- Outdated electrical service
- Broken windows

Structural /major issues

Any of the following issues with a property may be a deal-breaker for a beginning investor but could also signal an excellent opportunity for a more experienced investor. Regardless, one should proceed with caution.

- Foundation or walls
- Plumbing issues, including galvanized pipe, collapsed or cracked sewer line
- Leaning chimney
- Floors that slope
- Asbestos siding
- Rotting wood in the frame
- Lead paint

- Roof replacement: A roof may be serviceable but have two or three layers. If so, what will be the cost to replace the shingles?
- Buried underground oil tank
- Old furnace and/or central air unit
- Mold
- Major termite damage

As an investor, you should not expect to compete successfully with home buyers for properties that are in great condition. Buyers of owner-occupied properties will pay more for these properties, perhaps even above the seller's asking price.

In my experience, owner-occupied buyers are likely to walk away from properties that need work. These types of properties offer the best opportunity for good to great deals for real estate investors.

Minor repairs and updates can be handled by most investors, but if you are a new or inexperienced investor with no real construction knowledge, it's not a good idea to buy a property that has structural issues or will require major remodeling. In fact, if you were my client, I would probably advise you to wait for a property that will not require as much work.

Some people believe that real estate agents only care about receiving a commission check, but I can assure you that agents who work with investors understand that you are making a significant financial investment. Your agent should provide advice that is in your best interests, even when it means missing out on a sale.

What kinds of properties are likely to be excellent candidates for flipping or renting?

- Located in a desirable, family-friendly neighborhood
- Ugly duckling of the neighborhood

- Vacant properties tagged by the city for violations
- Absentee owner (research the county assessor's website)
- Properties that have character and charm
- Properties with unfinished basements
- Wood floors under the carpet
- Advertised as an estate sale
- Properties in any condition that have potential for increased value

Keep in mind that a property that needs work represents an opportunity for a savvy and knowledgeable investor. If you fall in love with the deal and not the property, you will never go wrong.

Here are a few easy and inexpensive ways to improve a property:

- Clean the house thoroughly, including the appliances.
- Paint the interior a nice neutral color.
- Replace linoleum with ceramic tile
- Replace old carpet (you can only clean it so often).
- Replace kitchen knobs if necessary, as well as old faucets.
- Rake the yard, trim bushes, cut the grass, and plant some flowers to ensure that the property is presentable and has excellent curb appeal.

These are simple things to do, and you can expect your property values to increase dramatically. If you invest 10 cents to make a dollar, it's a good investment.

Step 5: Sell/Rent

Obviously, by the time you get to this step, you have decided whether you want to rent the property or sell it. Not sure if you've put in enough work? Here are a couple of questions to ask yourself:

1. Would you let one of your relatives live in the property in its current condition?

2. Would you be proud enough to show the property to one of your best friends?

If your answer is yes, you are a proud property owner. Good for you.

Where can you advertise rental property?

Renting a property quickly is critical. The longer it takes to get the property rented, the lower the income for the investor.

- *Newspaper classified sections* (print and online) list rental properties, often in the weekend edition. This may not be the best option as newspaper ads can cost $25 to $50 or more.
- *Local bulletin boards* can be found at colleges, grocery stores, religious institutions, laundromats, and other locations.
- *Word of mouth* is an excellent way to connect with potential tenants. Let your good tenants know that you have additional rental properties available. They may have a relative, friend, or co-worker who is looking for a place to live.
- *Put a "For Rent" sign in the front yard.* If the property is located on a well-traveled road, hundreds of cars will drive by daily.
- *Work with a Realtor or property management company.* This is the most expensive way to advertise your property.

Regardless of how you decide to advertise your rental property, it is important to respond to queries right away because quality tenants will have many options available to them. If you do not contact them promptly, you will miss out. See the Resource section at the back of this book for a list of the best websites to advertise your rental.

How should you screen prospective tenants?

Careful selection of tenants will significantly improve your chances of succeeding in this business. The question you need to ask yourself is what type of tenant you want. I prefer a tenant commensurate with the quality and condition of the property.

Tenant screening services can help you determine whether someone is qualified to rent a property. Generally they will charge a fee equal to half a month's rent or more. See the Resources section for a list of the best tenant screening services.

Credit checks, criminal background checks, landlord verifications from two previous landlords, and employment verifications are critical.

Probably the least important of the various screening tools is the credit check. Keep in mind that if everyone had good credit, there would not be a rental business. Your gut instincts can also tell you a lot about a potential tenant.

Make sure to do your due diligence before handing over the keys to a new tenant. If you take shortcuts, you will regret it later. Take your time with each applicant and follow the same procedures with all applicants so you do not run into any discrimination problems. You should also become familiar with your local state's landlord-tenant laws.

Be aware that not all tenants will be honest about their backgrounds or past issues. The fact that they drive a nice car or wear nice clothes should not influence your decision. If they have cash for the first month's rent and deposit, a red flag should go up. It is also essential to confirm the information they provide on their previous landlord. Verify by going to your county assessor to see who the owner of the record is. Some people will write the name of a relative as their landlord. Of course, they will provide a stellar review even if the applicant was evicted.

A word of advice: You do not have to be a friend to your tenant, but it is your responsibility to be friendly and respectful.

Renting to anyone without verifying information will backfire. Careful tenant selection minimizes the risk that a property will be trashed.

A good tenant will leave the property in excellent condition. The opposite will occur with a poor tenant that no other landlord would rent to. Careful tenant selection determines whether this business will lead to success or failure.

When potential tenants call to view your rental, you should have a set of questions to ask that will help separate good prospects from bad ones. It will save you a lot of time if you do not show your property to tenants who do not meet your criteria. You must ask the same questions of all tenants so you are not accused of discrimination. See the Resources section for a list of sample questions to ask prospective tenants over the phone.

Is it important to require tenants to sign a lease?

Yes, because a lease ensures that there is no misunderstanding of responsibilities. A lease is a legal and binding contract that sets forth the landlord's and tenant's rights, duties, and responsibilities. A sample lease is provided in the Resources section. After both parties have signed the lease, both are bound by its terms.

What should a lease include?

1. Names of the tenant, the landlord or the landlord's agent, and the person or company authorized to manage the property.

2. Tenancy terms (will the lease be month to month or for a year or more?)

3. Address of the property and what appliances, if any, are included.

4. The amount of rent required, date when the monthly payment is due, any grace period, and any late charges or non-sufficient funds fees.

5. How the rent should be paid (check, money order, or cash).

6. Methods for terminating the agreement before the expiration date and what, if any, charges will be imposed.

7. The amount of the security deposit.

8. Whether the tenant or landlord pays for utilities.

9. Rules and regulations such as pet rules (pet deposit or pet rent), pest control, and many others.

10. Methods of resolving maintenance issues.

CHAPTER 8
THE GOOD, BETTER, BEST SCENARIO

Flipping is often portrayed as a complicated process by people who write books, present seminars, and charge ridiculous fees for their systems. Maybe you know someone who attended a flipping seminar and ended up spending thousands of dollars on information that was useless. Or maybe they hired a coach or mentor who did not even live in their community. In either case, they were spending money that could have been put to better use for a down payment or remodeling costs.

In talking with my clients about evaluating an investment property, I always suggest that they envision three different profit potential scenarios: good, better, and best.

A. The good price point is the highest price they should pay for the property and the lowest price at which it can be sold to make what they consider a good profit. For example, a property may have a purchase price of $80,000 and a selling price of $120,000, and the total expenses for repairs, selling costs, etc., are $30,000, producing a profit of $10,000 before taxes. How many hourly wage earners do you know who must work for three to four months to earn $10,000?

B. The better price point is the price they should pay for the property and the price at which it can be sold to make what they consider a better profit. Example: $75,000 purchase price, $125,000 selling price, $30,000 total expenses for repairs, selling costs, etc., producing $20,000 profit before taxes. How many hourly wage earners do you know who must work for five to eight months to earn $20,000?

C. The best price point is the lowest price they could pay for the property and the highest price at which it could be sold to make what they consider the best possible profit.

Example: $70,000 purchase price, $130,000 selling price, $30,000 total expenses for repairs, selling costs, etc., producing $30,000 profit before taxes. How many hourly wage earners do you know who must work a year or more to earn $30,000?

Planning is the most effective way to minimize risk. What if the property does not sell? This outcome is unlikely when you have these three scenarios in mind, but a property that does not sell can also become a rental unit. Instant equity is the result, and wealth-building is the outcome.

Holding on to a property for a more extended period has an additional benefit: the profit will be taxed at a lower rate. When a property is sold within the first year after purchase, the IRS treats the gain as ordinary income and taxes it at rates that can be too high, depending on your income tax bracket. If the property is held for more than one year after being purchased, the profits made by selling it are considered capital gains and are taxed at a rate that is typically lower than ordinary income.

As with any other aspect of real estate investment, people who are contemplating flipping properties or owning rental properties should seek the advice of a competent and knowledgeable accountant as well as a Realtor who has flipped a few properties.

SELLING TIME

Flipping should happen within a relatively short period. The longer a property is on the market, the less the profit will be because the investor is responsible for paying utilities, insurance, carrying costs, and so on until the property is sold.

CAPITAL REQUIREMENT

Although some people will say the major disadvantage of flipping is that you need a large amount of money to purchase and upgrade a property, I do not see this as a disadvantage. Anyone who is creditworthy can secure funds. Cash is always best, but investors can use other people's money (OPM) by opening a credit line, taking out a bridge loan, or pooling resources with a partner. Earning money by flipping does not have to be a fantasy. It is a reality for the clients I serve and for me.

Holding onto a rental property over the long term is an excellent way to build wealth. While the tenant reduces the debt, property values continue to go up, and residual income for the investor's retirement years is the outcome.

Note: The information on the Good, Better, Best scenario form in the Resources section can also be used as a guide to get a rough idea of how much equity you will have in the property. You already know how much you spent for expenses, and the only thing that remains is to estimate the value in each of the three categories. Your agent can provide you with comparable values to plug in. Let us say that the minimum sale price for a similar property is $120,000, the average sale price is $150,000, and the maximum sale price is $175.000. Plug in the total expenses, and that should give you the rough equity.

How should you decide whether to buy and flip or buy and hold? Here are a few things to consider:

1. What are you planning to do with the profits? Do you want to buy a car, take a vacation, pay off debt, pay for your children's college expenses, or use the funds for a down payment on your next flip or rental property?

2. Are you aware that your profits from flipping will be treated as ordinary income for tax purposes?

3. Is it better for you to earn income now (flipping) or residual
    income later (buy and hold)?

My FABFS/R system is no different from that used for purchasing properties to hold; however, you should not hesitate to
pay more for a long-term rental property because of the power
of leverage. Ultimately, the tenant is making your mortgage payment. Think about it: $10,000 at 5% interest on a 15-year loan
will cost you $39.54 per month. Will the rent cover this?

Flipping is all about the bottom line: Will the property produce enough profit to make the project worthwhile? I have successfully flipped many properties using the good, better, best scenario rather than wasting my money on costly systems.

The Good, Better, Best scenario form and the remodeling es-
timator will be your safety net and will answer the question "Will
this flip will make enough money?"

CHAPTER 9
FLIPPING STRATEGIES

If you are planning to flip a property, what steps should you take to improve it before putting it on the market?

Keep in mind that most of your remodeling budget should be devoted to updating the kitchen and bath(s). Does that mean you should install granite counters instead of Formica? It depends on the price point.

What about replacing kitchen cabinets versus painting? Again, it depends on the price point of the expected sale.

Remodeling does not have to be expensive. It is unnecessary to hire a high-end contractor who is likely to make more money than you will. Your goal should be to improve the property's overall appeal and market value, thereby increasing the profit margin.

Across the country in 2020, home flips dropped about 13% from 2019 to the lowest level since 2016. In 2020 a total of 241,630 single-family homes and condos across the United States were purchased and resold, mostly by investors looking to make a profit. ATTOM Data counts a flip as any property sale that was an arm's length transaction that occurred in the quarter where a previous arm's length transaction on the same property had occurred within the last 12 months. (Source: RISMedia.com.)

HOW MUCH SHOULD YOU SPEND TO IMPROVE A PROPERTY?

If your remodeling efforts cost $25,000 and the property's value will only increase by $18,000, perhaps this would be a better wholesaling project than a flipper. Wholesaling allows you to sell the property to another investor and make money without doing anything to it. On the other hand, if the remodeling cost will be $18,000 and increase the property's value by $25,000, the fix-up project should move forward. There is no reason to spend $1 to make $1. Paying 50 cents to make $1 makes a lot more sense.

You must weigh the remodeling costs (including time and effort) against the profit potential. If the project will make the property more appealing to a potential buyer and not cut into the profit, then it may be a great way to make an excellent return on the property investment.

The best way to increase a home's value without overspending is to do exactly what needs doing and nothing more. Making the necessary improvements will increase the property's value and make it more attractive to a buyer.

There are numerous simple things you can do to increase the value of a property:

1. Pay attention to curb appeal. An excellent first impression can dramatically increase the value of the property.

2. Take care of landscaping and yard work (mowing, trimming, and weeding). The yard is the first thing potential buyers will see. Planting flowers is an inexpensive way to make a property more appealing.

3. Remove old carpet and refinish hardwood floors.

4. Refinish or reface kitchen cabinets and replace knobs. Replace lighting fixtures in the kitchen ceiling.

5. Paint interior/exterior.

6. Remodel bathroom(s).

LISTING AND SELLING A RENOVATED PROPERTY

Ideally, the agent who helped you buy the property should be the one who lists it for you when you are ready to sell. If you try to sell it without involving your agent, they will not want to do business with you the next time you go to them for help, and they will not be interested in helping you find good deals.

To sell quickly, the listing price should be lower than the asking price for similar properties in the same neighborhood. Since you should be looking at the bottom line instead of being emotional in making these decisions, a few thousand dollars plus or minus will not be a big issue.

SIX FLIPPING STRATEGIES:

1. *Buy, fix, flip retail market:* This strategy involves fixing a property and selling it to a homeowner. It is the most profitable flipping strategy and also the most time-consuming.

2. *Buy and flip "as is":* This strategy involves doing minimal work (which could be as simple as cleaning up the property) and then selling it in its current condition to another investor.

3. *Buy and flip wholesale without doing any work:* This strategy involves acquiring a property at a low price and selling it below market value to another investor. It is not unusual to make $5,000 to $15,000 this way.

4. *Wholesaling:* This is an opportunity for individuals to make money without having any skin in the game. They generally write a purchase agreement and the seller thinks the property is sold, but then they do an assignment for a profit with a buyer who will close on the property. As a Realtor I am not a big fan of this strategy.

5. *Flip to a long-term rental.* The Good, Better, Best scenario form will give you an idea how much equity you would have. Your agent can provide you with comps for the active, pending, and sold properties in the area.

6. *Flip your own house:* To use this strategy, you must live in the property at least two of the previous five years before selling it.

   If you are single, you can make up to $250,000 tax-free.

   If you are married, you and your spouse can make up to $500,000 tax-free.

   This strategy is especially good for a young couple who are interested in buying their first home, because they can buy a property that needs work and do the renovations while living in the house.

   I have personally used Strategy 6 four to five times in a row. It is an excellent way to start a real estate investment business because you can use the money from flipping as a down payment on the next property and finance the rest.

WHAT CAN YOU DO WITH THE MONEY FROM FLIPPING?

Here are a few ideas:

1. Pay off credit card debt. This is worthwhile even if you must pay ordinary income tax on the profit from flipping. It is hard to think about wealth building when one is in debt.

2. Pay for a college education for yourself or your children. I paid for two of my kids to attend the University of Kansas.

3. Reward yourself for hard work by taking an amazing vacation.

4. Buy a newer car (I did not say "new car" because a brand-new car will depreciate as soon as you drive it off the lot).

5. Some people, such as yours truly, have even used flipping to pay for a life cycle event called alimony.

Would you like to be your boss and have the independence to do as you wish? Most logical people want to control their destiny, and in my opinion, the ticket to financial independence is investing in real estate. Building wealth by investing in one property at a time is within your reach.

The most important advice I can give you is to stick to your strategy and keep on doing it over and over if you are making money. While you can flip any type of real estate, my focus with the 150+ properties I flipped was houses and a couple of duplexes. It became extremely easy for me because I use the same interior and exterior paint, the same flooring, tile, countertops, bathroom fixtures, etc.

I know my market and what renovations are necessary to do. There is no reason to do more than you must, as it will eat up your bottom line.

Using the FABFS/R system works. There is no reason to speculate. It is a proven system that has served me very well.

CHAPTER 10
DOES YOUR AGENT HAVE WHAT IT TAKES?

To succeed as a real estate investor, you need to work with the right agent. Your real estate agent should be your coach, mentor, consultant, and wealth advisor, and you should feel confident that they will always have your best interests in mind.

Is your current agent have experienced in this specialized area? Experience with helping people from all walks of life to buy and sell a personal residence is not good enough. Their real estate license gives them the opportunity to represent buyers and sellers in a transaction, but it does not give them the expertise to help you make good investment decisions.

Your agent should be able to say something like this: "I represent people who buy and sell houses, but I am also an investor and investment specialist who helps people generate wealth and retirement income. In other words, I mentor, coach, and serve as a consultant and wealth advisor to my clients."

Never forget that you are investing your hard-earned money; therefore, your agent should know a lot more than you do. It's not enough to work with an agent just because you like them and trust them.

> My idea of an investor-friendly real estate agent is one who sees things others do not see... one who has an eye for an opportunity — for spotting "the deal."

Here is another way to put it. Real estate agents have different credentials, just as doctors do. If you have a problem with your heart, would you make an appointment with an oncologist or gynecologist? No. You would seek out a cardiologist. Would you want to find out about your cardiologist's training and credentials?

The same should apply to the real estate industry. Does the agent under consideration have the credentials you are looking for?

WHAT SHOULD YOU EXPECT FROM YOUR AGENT?

If you intend to invest in real estate, your agent should be able to do the following things to ensure they will bring added value to you:

- Know and understand your goals.
- Have a basic understanding of tax considerations.
- Understand different types of investment properties and be able to analyze a property to determine whether it will be a good investment or not.
- Ideally, control a sizable portfolio and have experience flipping properties.
- Be able to explain the advantages and disadvantages of the real estate investment choices available to you.
- Understand 1031 exchanges and 401(K), self-directed, and Roth IRAs.
- Be familiar with local property values and comparable properties.
- Know how to search the MLS for deals.
- Maintain strong relationships with local banks, lenders, and others who deal with investors.
- Know the landlord/tenant laws of your state (http://www.thelpa.com/lpa/lllaw.html).

Bottom line: To be taken seriously as a real estate consultant or wealth advisor, your agent will need to provide services that other real estate agents do not offer. Their skills should set them apart from other real estate agents who lack this knowledge. They should be able to help you every step of the way to accomplish your objectives.

If your current agent lacks the expertise you need, why are you using them? Unless they took an investment class, their real estate training did not prepare them to work with investors. Most real estate agents lack this knowledge, and maybe that is why so few agents understand that real estate is one of the best investment options to generate wealth.

If you have never met any agents who specialize in real estate investment, contact the brokers of the top two or three real estate agencies in your community and ask them to recommend an agent who has the knowledge you are looking for.

The top producer at an agency will not necessarily be the right person for you to work with. If they don't own even one rental property, they would be of no help to you. You need to find out if they are working with investors regularly and how many investment properties they have sold; otherwise, you can do better.

I am not sure how many agents in your community would fit this description, but if you look hard enough you will find the right one. Some agents (including me) make a terrific living by helping clients build wealth and retirement income, but they also do a fair amount of business with owner-occupied buyers. I bring added value because I am an active investor who understands the ins and outs of this business. I have flipped a lot of houses, so I am practicing what I recommend that others should do.

With all the benefits that real estate offers, I was surprised to read in an industry publication recently that less than 3% of real estate agents own at least one investment property. That is a very shocking number. I cannot understand why so many agents do not invest in their own industry.

Your agent should take you seriously

If you are fortunate to find a rock star real estate agent who meets your criteria, they will be highly sought after. Don't take this personally, but they must gather enough information to see if you will be a good fit for them. On the other hand, you will also need to determine whether you want to do business with them.

As you know, not every person who wants to invest in real estate will have the right motives or the financial wherewithal to get started. While this may not apply to you, some people are vulnerable to get-rich-quick schemes and empty promises. Your focus should be on building a long-term relationship with an agent and following a business plan to build wealth and retirement income over the long term. You want your agent to take you seriously enough to devote time and energy to helping you.

I am confident that you want to do business with an agent who has integrity and is loyal and trustworthy. As an agent, I also want to do business with clients with the same attributes so I need to find out as much as possible before working with them. It makes sense to know and learn about their goals and aspirations, and they should know the same things about me. Later in this chapter you'll find a list of suggested questions to ask an agent.

AGENTS SHOULD BE AN ADVOCATE FOR THEIR INDUSTRY

If your financial advisor does not own any investment properties, they are unlikely to be bullish on real estate. What is their compensation for recommending real estate?

Are there better ways to make money while minimizing risk? I agree that it makes sense to be diversified, but I have not found a better option than real estate investing.

Agents make a living by helping clients buy and sell their personal residences, but they can generate wealth by investing in real estate and helping people like yourself do the same. Here is the bottom line: When they do not own real estate, it is tough to provide the guidance people like you and others should expect.

If agents understand that working with people like you and others can be one of the most critical aspects of their business, it will be a win-win for them to work with you. When they help you accomplish your goals, you will be more likely to tell others about them.

WHY DO SOME REAL ESTATE AGENTS CHOOSE TO WORK WITH INVESTORS?

Since I got my real estate license in 1998, I have sold a lot of properties for my clients and bought and sold a fair amount of my own properties. I continue to do a fair amount of business, yet I do not consider myself better than other agents.

My business has not grown because I did phone duty or was lucky but because I am an investor with the credentials to help clients generate wealth. I have the mindset of an investor instead of a real estate agent.

Some agents may have worked with one or more investors in the past but did not enjoy the experience. Maybe they would rather work with clients who are likely to buy an expensive home instead of investors who are looking for a deal.

Many agents in every real estate company work hard and are knowledgeable and experienced but are struggling to make a living. They are always looking for more clients. Why are they missing out on potential income by overlooking clients who are investors?

Some agents have discovered that investors have great potential for repeat business. A buyer of owner-occupied property may utilize their agent's services every five to seven years if they are lucky, while investors will use their agent over and over if he or she can bring them deals that make sense.

One of the most rewarding referrals I ever received has been my client since 2005. That same client has purchased more than 300 properties in the past sixteen years. One year he made $300,000 by flipping properties.

I have found that investors are not as emotional as home buyers. Many times, they will write an offer on the spot. A 10-minute showing can result in an accepted offer.

Investors are not as concerned about minor cosmetic details as owner-occupied buyers are. Their focus is on the financial numbers and whether they can make money from their investment by flipping it or holding it as a long-term rental.

It is not necessary for an agent to work with a lot of investors. They need to work with the right ones who have the financial wherewithal to continue investing. In comparison with homeowners who buy one property at a time, investor clients will keep their agent busy writing many offers. The agent will not have to spend time waiting for the phone to ring or doing open houses.

I have found that working with investors is not only financially rewarding but also profoundly satisfying. When I have earned their trust, they will listen to my advice and feel grateful to me for helping them make a good living and build wealth. Often I am bringing them more value than their financial planner or stockbroker does. I do not have to negotiate my commission because they know that I have helped them make money.

Investors should expect their agent to find deals for them on the MLS or through other sources even before the properties are listed. Their agent should resist writing ridiculous lowball offers. The seller will probably receive multiple offers, including higher than the asking price, so a low offer will likely be rejected.

My suggestion is to listen to your agent's advice because if you do not, they will feel that you are unreasonable and will decide not to continue working with you. Keep in mind that an agent who has knowledge and expertise in investment is extremely valuable. You must be reasonable with your expectations as well.

If they are an agent with a busy practice, their time is precious. Do not waste it by asking them to write ridiculous offers that will never materialize.

YOUR AGENT WILL BE YOUR PATH TO SUCCESS

You should feel confident that your agent will be the quickest path to accomplish your objectives. You should see them as your mentor, coach, and wealth builder.

They should know the neighborhoods in your city or town and be familiar with property values. They should know where to find an undervalued property. Loyalty is essential to them, and it should be to you as well because if they have a sizeable client base, their challenge is to decide which client to call first when they find out about a great deal.

I believe a knowledgeable agent should be the most essential member of your team. Here are some points to keep in mind:

1. Your agent should understand the process of investing in real estate. It helps if they are also an investor (even on a small scale) because it means they have gone through the process.

2. They should be comfortable writing multiple offers. However, you should listen to them if they tell you that writing low-ball offers is a waste of time.

3. They should have experience helping others like you. You want to feel confident that you are in good hands because you will be making your most significant financial investments ever.

4. They should have a good reputation for helping investors succeed. Success breeds success. When they do an excellent job for you, why would you not be willing to refer them to your friends and others? Most of my clients have come to me through referrals.

5. They should be honest with you. They should be able to tell
    you whether a property makes sense financially. If you in-
    tend to flip the property, will the profits be enough to make
    it worthwhile?

6. They should behave with integrity and do the right thing
    instead of focusing on their next commission check.

7. They should find properties that meet your needs and ob-
    jectives. For example, cash flow is more important to some
    buyers than to others. They should know and understand
    what you are looking for.

8. They should understand your preferences. Most investors will
    write offers with the same terms each time, such as cash, close
    in a short time, contractor/inspector contingency.

9. They should not waste your time by sending you properties
    that do not meet your criteria.

10. They should have some knowledge regarding your local
    investors or property owners association.

11. They should meet with you at least annually to determine
    whether your properties are still meeting your needs.

12. They should stay in touch with you and send you articles
    of interest and be your ongoing source for all of your real
    estate investment needs.

In advising you, they should always keep your best interests
in mind. If they are too excited, aggressive, or desperate, they
could push you to make bad decisions. If they are too conserva-
tive, you could miss an opportunity. Remember that your money
is not theirs, so they should not use the word "we" unless they
have a vested interest in the transaction. Saying "my client" is
much better than saying "we" when discussing a potential deal.

I hope you find an agent who meets your needs, is knowledgeable and trustworthy, and will always have your back. Even if you are tempted to go at this alone, remember that your agent can help you get to your destination much faster.

YOUR AGENT CAN BRING ADDED VALUE IN THE FOLLOWING WAYS:

1. Suggest sources of financing. Recommend banks that are friendly and are willing to loan money on investment properties with favorable terms. In my experience, local /community banks are much easier to work with than nationwide banks such as US Bank, Bank of the West, or Wells Fargo.

2. Provide information that will help you decide whether an undervalued property is a good deal. They should be able to provide an estimate of the potential rent for the property under consideration.

3. Recommend other professionals who specialize in real estate, including lawyers, accountants, contractors, and property managers.

4. Be prepared to handle many details after the offer has been accepted (such as contractor inspections, home inspections, termite inspections, and surveys).

5. Provide information about what is going on in your marketplace, including neighborhoods that may be improving or declining.

6. Suggest things you can do to increase a property's value.

SAMPLE QUESTIONS TO ASK AGENTS YOU ARE INTERVIEWING:

- How long have you been an agent? Are you working with investors? What is your investment philosophy?
- Do you own any rental properties? Are they houses, duplexes, apartments, or commercial buildings? What type of property do you prefer, and what has been your overall experience so far?
- Are you working with any investors now? How many investors are you working with? (It does not matter how many, but it is important that they have some experience.)
- How many transactions have you done? Are the transactions mainly houses?
- Are you working with any investors that have flipped houses? Have you flipped houses yourself?
- How many investment properties have you sold in the past? What types of properties have you sold?
- What types of multi-units have you sold?
- Do you have any knowledge of the commercial real estate market?
- Do you know any bankers or lenders who are familiar with investment properties?
- Do you have a list of contractors that you could recommend?
- Do you have a list of references from clients?
- What are some of the neighborhoods you would recommend?
- Tell me about the advantages or disadvantages of investing in houses, duplexes, apartments, and so on.
- What have been your overall experiences in working with investors?

Keep in mind that the agent you are interviewing will also be interested in your background and readiness level, so they should be asking you pertinent questions as well. Hopefully, their responses to your questions will give you confidence that you will be in excellent hands with them.

In conclusion, my advice to you is to be loyal to your agent and use them exclusively. Why should they be loyal to you and call you about a good deal if you are not loyal to them?

CHAPTER 11
HOW WILL YOU BUY?

Early on in your process, you should know how you intend to purchase a property. The decision to finance or pay cash will determine your return on investment, so finding the best financing option is critical.

As previously mentioned, if you are creditworthy, have a solid financial statement, and are employed, you have a fantastic opportunity even in today's competitive market to acquire a sizable portfolio. If you are self-employed, it may be a bit more challenging to obtain financing, so make sure that you can provide at least the two latest tax returns.

Although some real estate "gurus" have proclaimed that people can buy a property with no credit, poor credit, or no job, would you sell a property you own that is in a family-friendly neighborhood to someone who has no credit? If a seller has a rundown property in an undesirable area that they cannot sell any other way, however, this may be their only option.

If you are using a real estate agent, can you imagine a seller being willing to sell a property with no money down yet pay a commission out of pocket? I have never met anyone who bought a property that was worth owning with no money down. Does it happen? It probably happens on rare occasions, but the message that anyone can purchase property with no money down is highly unrealistic.

In many instances, I have paid cash for a property or used a line of credit to purchase the property and cover fix-up costs. Once the work was completed, the bank appraised the property and I was able to refinance for the exact amount of money I had invested. In effect, this was a "no money down" proposition that was available to me because I was creditworthy.

The key is that I bought an undervalued property, and even after the fix-up cost, the loan-to-value ratio was 60% of the appraised value—not a very risky proposition for the bank. This type of scenario can happen regularly, but if one is not credit-worthy or does not have a solid financial statement, it is unlikely to take place.

Have you established meaningful relationships with your local or community bank or other financing sources such as credit unions? Keep in mind that banks are in the business of loaning money, so this is a win-win situation for you and them. Ideally, you want a lender who understands the real estate investment market. If they lack this knowledge, you can try to educate them or find another lender that will better meet your needs.

I have found that local institutions, including community banks, are much easier to deal with than nationwide banks, especially for lines of credit and commercial-type loans.

As you already know, investors prefer to use OPM (other people's money) as much as possible, so establishing good relationships with bankers and other lenders is critical.

DIFFERENT WAYS TO PURCHASE PROPERTIES

1. Cash or line of credit – Most of the investors I work with pay for their purchases by using a line of credit (LOC) that works the same as cash. They use the LOC to purchase a property, make the necessary improvements, get the property appraised, and then term it out with permanent financing. The majority term out the loan at their local community bank with a "commercial loan" amortized over 10 to 20 years with a 5- to 7-year balloon. Loans like this are much easier to secure than a traditional mortgage. Keep in mind that if you use a mortgage broker, they will follow Fannie Mae guidelines that limit the number of properties you can buy.

The same process can be used if you intend to flip rather than use the property as a rental. Once the property is sold, the LOC is paid back. This is the preferred method because the seller does not have to be concerned about appraisals.

2. *Commercial loan* – These types of loans are typically used for large projects such as apartments, office buildings, and residential properties above four units. Underwriting in the commercial market focuses more on the property than on the income of the borrower. If you are interested in purchasing a $5,000,000 apartment building, the lender will want to make sure that the income it produces will support the mortgage payment if anything goes wrong. The lender will still want to ensure that you are creditworthy, and this type of loan is not likely to be issued to a first-time investor.

3. *Conventional mortgage* – What else can I say about conventional financing that you do not already know? You may not be aware that some lenders require more than the usual 20% down payment. In fact, the required down payment can be as high as 30% to 35%. It is best to check with several lenders, as some may offer special down payment programs for investors.

4. *Family, friends, and other individuals* – This form of financing is unique because of the relationship between the lender and borrower. Family members may pool their financial resources to invest as a "family activity." As another example, a family member may have discretionary funds such as $100,000 in the bank earning little interest but could do much better by loaning the money for a set period and receiving a 5% to 7% return.

5. *Partnership* – Partnerships come in all forms. I have two partners in my real estate business. All three of us are equal partners who share in profits and expenses. You might know someone who would be willing to take an ownership position but would not want to be directly involved in the project. Partners receive tax benefits based on their percentage of the investment (cash flow, appreciation, depreciation, and so on) as well as their share of the profits when the property is sold.

6. *FHA loan* – FHA loans are accessible to buyers who may not have enough money for a down payment on a conventional mortgage because the minimum down payment on an FHA loan is only 3.5 percent. An FHA loan can be used to purchase an investment property up to four units if the purchaser plans to live in one of the units. This is an excellent strategy if you do not have a lot of money besides the down payment.

7. *FHA 203k loan* – This type of loan can be used to purchase a property that needs rehabbing. You can use the money to finance repairs and other improvements. The 203k loan is available if you plan to occupy at least one of the units.

8. *Seller financing* – In some instances, it may be advantageous for a seller to partially finance the property, primarily if it is owned free and clear. I have not seen much seller financing in a very long time. If you find a seller who is willing to do this, you should seek the advice of an attorney to draw up the documents.

9. *Hard money lender* – If traditional financing is not obtainable, hard money lenders may offer a temporary solution. Any private individual can be a hard money lender. This type of loan is based on property value. The loan term is usually three to six months, and the interest

rate is extremely high: 10 to 20 percent. Hard money lenders charge high fees for loans. In addition to paying the high cost of these loans, a borrower who cannot meet the deadline for repayment may face foreclosure or must pay additional fees to renew the loan.

Although most investors rely on options 1–3, the preferred option is number 1. The other options may be helpful if you cannot finance your purchase through traditional means. You also might want to consider using funds from a Roth IRA to finance real estate purchases.

WHY IS REFINANCING AN EXCELLENT STRATEGY FOR BUILDING WEALTH?

It does not make sense to pay cash to purchase a rental property unless you term it out because it would cause you to miss out on one of the most significant tax benefits of real estate ownership—the interest deduction.

Let us say you pay $100,000 for a property in cash with no intent to refinance. If the property goes up in value by $10,000, what is the return on the investment in the first year? 10%. Another way of looking at it would be to calculate the cash-on-cash return after year one. For this purpose, let us say the annual cash flow before taxes is $3,525. Your cash-on-cash return is $3525/$100,000 = 3.525%.

Now let us say instead of paying for the $100,000 property with cash, you put down $20,000. If the property value goes up by $10,000, what is the return on investment in the first year? 50%. If the annual cash flow before taxes is $3,525, your cash-on-cash return is $3525/$20,000 = 17.62%.

The numbers speak for themselves. Can you now see the power of leverage?

When you have your finances in order, you will be well on your way to achieving success in this business. Your agent will take you seriously and help you accomplish your wealth-building objectives.

CHAPTER 12
PUTTING IT ALL TOGETHER

The strategies described in this book have worked well for me during my nearly five decades as an investor and over 2 decades as a real estate agent. The financial benefits of my real estate investment business have been substantial, but money has not been the only reward I have received from investing in real estate and working with investors. My life has also been enriched through longtime friendships with many of my former clients, tenants, and colleagues.

If you have been sitting on the sidelines while others are reaping the financial benefits of investing in real estate, I hope reading this book has helped you decide to get in the "game." You now have knowledge and hopefully, the confidence to make your real estate investment business very lucrative for you and your family.

PUT YOUR NEWFOUND KNOWLEDGE TO USE

You are now able to do more than just talk about investing. You have enough knowledge to take the necessary steps. Remember that wealth is found on the other side of fear.

- You should know your short- and long-term objectives.
- You know how to make good business decisions.
- You can identify properties that have investment potential.
- You can analyze whether a property is likely to be a poor, good, or great investment. (Remember that price alone will not tell you whether a property is a good deal.)
- You should be able to connect with contractors, property management companies, bankers, accountants, attorneys, and people in the trades.

Armed with this knowledge, the sky is now the limit. You must decide how far you want to go in your real estate investment business. It can be   extremely rewarding financially. Your strategy can include a mix of buy-and-hold or buy-and-flip, and either option can help you enjoy the financially security you deserve in the years to come.

Although great deals are no longer as readily available today as they were in the past, they can still be found. If finding these deals is part of your overall business plan and goals, you will succeed.

You now understand the different strategies for buy-and-hold versus buy-and-flip. Additionally, you are familiar with some of the tax benefits available to you. Of course, you should always seek the advice of a competent accountant who ideally is an investor as well. Getting the right advice can ensure that you will pay no more than your fair share of taxes.

Armed with all of this knowledge, you will be able to enjoy the benefits this industry has to offer.

An action plan for success

Believe in yourself, and don't listen to the pundits. Know that your real estate investments can generate wealth and retirement income, perhaps much more than you achieved from other non-real-estate investments. Remember that real estate is one of the better vehicles for wealth building and one of the few options that can provide tax benefits.

The mistake I have seen most often is that many investors think they can do this on their own. In my opinion, working with the right real estate agent is the quickest way to accomplish your financial objectives. I would strongly encourage you to be extremely loyal to your agent, and you should expect the same loyalty from your agent. Since agents are independent contractors, they have a vested interest in finding properties that meet your needs so they can earn a commission. The relationship between a real estate investor and a real estate agent is the classical example of a WIN-WIN partnership.

As I mentioned at the beginning of this book, the real estate industry is filled with get-rich-quick programs that make big promises and never deliver. There are no secrets in this business that are worth asking someone to pay $10,000 or more to attend a seminar.

Never underestimate the influence your agent can have as your coach, mentor, and advisor. They won't charge a dime for their services when representing you as a buyer's agent. Who knows more about your community—you or someone who comes to town for a one-night stand and leaves the next day?

The actions you take during the next 30 days could change your life. (You can use the "30-day Action Plan Worksheet" and in the Resources section to get started.)

Knowledge is powerful, and you now have enough expertise to succeed and grow your business.

> Your pundits do not have the power to direct your financial future or your long-term wealth. You have taken the first steps to becoming independent, and do not have to listen to negativity. Only you can crush the naysayers and follow your own dreams.

As you know, any real estate agent can look on the MLS to find properties and open doors. Your agent should also be able to help you use the formulas for determining Net Operating Income, Cap Rates, Cash Flow Before Taxes, and Cash on Cash. They can tell you about properties that are not even listed.

Always keep in mind that when you achieve your goals, your agent will also achieve theirs

You are well on your way, and I wish you much success. If I can do it, so can you.

Congratulations on your decision to become a real estate investor! Drop me an email or call me at 402-679-3914 to ask questions or let me know what you thought of this book. Your feedback will be appreciated.

My email address is <u>reinvestorsclientsforlife@gmail.com</u>

RESOURCES

- ▶ 30-Day Action Plan Worksheet
- ▶ 1031 Exchange—Converting Investment Property to Your Primary Residence
- ▶ Business Plan (Sample)
- ▶ Cost Recovery (Depreciation)
- ▶ Analysis Case Study for Running the Numbers
- ▶ Formulas for Running the Numbers
- ▶ Property Analysis Buy and Hold Instructions
- ▶ Property Analysis Buy and Hold (Blank)
- ▶ Property Analysis Buy and Hold (Sample)
- ▶ Sample Interview Questions to Ask Tenants Over the Phone
- ▶ Lease Agreement (Sample)
- ▶ Tenant Screening Questions That Are Off-Limits
- ▶ Tenant Screening Services
- ▶ Websites for Advertising Your Rental Property
- ▶ Make-Ready Checklist for Rental Property (Between Tenants)
- ▶ Rehab Worksheet (Blank)
- ▶ Rehab Worksheet (Sample)
- ▶ Remodeling Worksheet
- ▶ Property Checklist
- ▶ Statement of Assets and Liabilities

30-DAY ACTION PLAN WORKSHEET

30-DAY ACTION PLAN WORKSHEET

Name:

MY ANNUAL GOAL   YEAR _____

MY MONTHLY GOAL   MONTH_____

MY ONE-MONTH GOAL

WEEK 1	WEEK 2	WEEK 3	WEEK 4

1031 EXCHANGE:
CONVERTING INVESTMENT PROPERTY
TO YOUR PRIMARY RESIDENCE

Exclusion of Gain from Sale of Residence

Many people are aware that they can sell their primary residence and not pay taxes on a significant amount of gain. Under Section 121 of the Internal Revenue Code, you will not owe capital gains taxes on up to $250,000 of gain or $500,000 of gain if you are married and filing jointly, when you sell a home that you used as your primary residence for at least two of the previous five years. Taxpayers can take advantage of this exclusion once every two years.

Property Converted from Investment to Primary Residence

Taxpayers used to be able to trade into a rental, rent the home for a while, move into it, and then exclude all or some of the gain under Section 121. Provided they lived in the home as their primary residence for at least two years, they could sell it and exclude the gain under Section 121 up to the maximum level of $250,000/$500,000. In recent years Congress amended Section 121 in order to limit the benefits of Section 121 when the property has also been used as a rental.

First, if you acquire property in a 1031 exchange and then convert it to your primary residence, you must own it at least five years before being eligible for the Section 121 exclusion.

Second, the amount of gain that you can exclude will be reduced to the extent that the house was used for something other than a primary residence during the period of ownership. The exclusion is reduced pro rata by comparing the number of years the property is used for non-primary residence purposes to the total number of years the property is owned by the taxpayer.

For example, a married couple uses a tax deferred exchange under Section 1031 to acquire a house as investment property. The couple rents the house for three years, and then moves into it and uses it as their primary residence for the next three years. The couple sells the property at the end of year 6, netting a total gain of $800,000. Instead of being able to exclude $500,000, the couple will not be able to exclude some of the gain based on how many years they rented the house. Since they rented it for three years out of six, 50% of the gain, or $400,000, will not be able to be excluded. Because of this new limitation, the couple will be able to exclude $400,000 of the gain rather than $500,000.

Exceptions

There are a couple exceptions to this restriction. If the house was used as a rental prior to January 1, 2009, the exclusion is not affected. Using the example provided above, if the three-year rental period occurred prior to January 1, 2009, the exclusion would not be reduced, and the couple would be able to exclude the full $500,000.

Another important exception is that property that is first used as a primary residence and later converted to investment property is not affected by these restrictions on excluding gain. For example, if you own and live in a house for 18 years and then you move out and rent the house for two years before selling it, you can receive the full amount of the exclusion. Because your investment use occurred after the last day of use as a primary residence, all the gain accumulated over your 20-year ownership of the property can be excluded, up to $250,000, or $500,000 for married couples.

Combining Exclusion with 1031 Exchange

Fortunately, the rules are favorable to taxpayers who are looking to combine Section 1031 with Section 121 to both exclude and defer tax when the property starts out as a primary residence and then is converted into an investment property. Provided the personal use occurs first, you can exclude gain under Section 121, and then defer tax on the remaining gain, provided you comply with the requirements of both Section 1031 and Section 121.

The Internal Revenue Code still provides investors with favorable options for exclusion of gain and tax deferral. The rules can be complicated, but with the right planning taxpayers can still make the most of their real estate investments.

References: Internal Revenue Code §121; Housing Assistance Tax Act of 2008 (H.R. 3221).

BUSINESS PLAN (SAMPLE)

20___ Real Estate Business Plan for Mr./Ms. Smart Investor

Specially Prepared for Jim Slick, Vice President of We Want Your Business Bank

BUSINESS GOALS

Mission

Our mission is to create income by purchasing undervalued properties to remodel, sell or retain as a long-term investment.

Mr. Smart Investor has over seven years of experience as an investor and is a Mortgage Broker with Last Chance Mortgage. He currently has a rental portfolio of ten single homes, five duplexes, and one five-plex.

Profit will be generated by:

1.) Performing cosmetic improvements to single-family homes and selling them to generate 40–50% profit.

2.) Maintaining long-term rentals that generate a minimum of 10% cash on cash return.

Short-Term Goals

We will create and uphold a reputation in our community for honesty in our business dealings, and we will aim to achieve win-win results.

We will focus on acquiring distressed properties that can be fixed and sold or used as rentals.

During _____, we will purchase five properties to flip and five properties to rent. This will be the beginning of our long-term investment strategy to accumulate income-producing properties.

An actual number of properties purchased in 20___:

flipped: 3   sold: 2   rentals: 3

Long-Term Goals

Our objective in _____ and each year after that until _____ will be to purchase an average of five properties per year to fix and sell and five properties per year to increase our rental portfolio.

Pursuing this strategy over five years will add 30 properties to our portfolio (single-family dwellings and duplexes) to go along with the 25 units currently in our portfolio (mix of single-family homes and multi-units, each returning an average of $3,000 positive annual cash flow for a total income of $75,000 per year and yearly asset appreciation of 3%.

During these five years, our objective is that more than 30 properties will be sold for an average of $15,000 profit each, for a total of more than $450,000 cash income.

OWNERSHIP

Want To Be Wealthy LLC

We intend to be highly leveraged. Licensed contractors will do all renovations.

DEVELOPING KNOWLEDGE OF THE MARKETPLACE

Target Neighborhoods

We will operate in the Midtown, Benson, and Northeast and Southeast part of the Omaha Metro area. These areas were chosen because properties can be purchased in the price range of $50,000 to $60,000 and our significant area knowledge.

Selecting Properties

We have developed a strategy involving purchases in the $50,000 to $60,000 price range. This price represents the lower end of what properties are selling for in the area, at least 20 to 40% less than average.

1. $30,000 between our purchase price and the typical sales price is necessary to achieve our profit margin of approximately $15,000.

2. For our rental portfolio, a purchase price of at least 20–40% price differential from market value is necessary for each purchase.

   These properties should be 3-bedrooms for resale and a minimum of 2-bedrooms for rentals to appeal to homeowners and renters.

   Properties should be located close to schools and shopping and should include amenities that will attract young families and first-time buyers.

Locating Flexible/Distressed Sellers

Our target market will be highly motivated sellers and may be having financial difficulties or those whose properties have been on the market for at least 3–4 months.

Properties that initially will meet our criteria include:

1. Foreclosures

2. Properties in disrepair

3. Property management problems

4. Estate sales

5. Absentee ownership

6. Tenant problems

7. Retirement or relocation

It is anticipated that these sellers will negotiate to meet our minimum purchase criteria.

DEVELOPING A NETWORK

To be successful with our strategy, we will establish a strong partnership with other agents, banks, and others.

BUSINESS OPERATIONS

Target Customer

The age group of 25–44 years.

1. Resale Properties

Our target buyer is a young, dual-income family. These buyers will have adequate credit but may lack significant cash reserves for a down payment or closing costs—the purchase price in the $100,000 to $120,000 price range.

Our approach to these buyers will be to utilize creative solutions to their cash shortage by using programs such as FHA, VA, and others.

2. Rentals

Our tenants' target market will include students, young couples, single parents, and dual-income families for our rental portfolio.

The target rent will be $650 to $900 per month. These tenants would also serve as perfect candidates to purchase the property in the future.

Performing Market Analysis

The source we will use to determine the value of a property will be market analysis available through Multiple Listing Service and our experience over the past seven years.

Financial Analysis

Each property to be purchased will be analyzed to determine the property's value, reasonable purchase price, estimated cost of renovation, acquisition costs, potential sale price, and anticipated profit.

Financial Arrangements

We have established relationships with the following banks:

We Want Your Business Badly, Yes We Can, First Preference, Last Resort Banks so we will know in advance of our ability to purchase properties that meet our criteria. As we will only purchase undervalued properties, after the renovations are completed, we will seek permanent financing based on the appraisal.

Renovation Process

We intend to purchase properties that are sold well below market value and require minimal cosmetic updates and improvements.

We anticipate that every property will require at least some cosmetic improvements to increase its value. We intend to sell these properties within 90 to 120 days, encompassing acquisition, remodeling, and purchase by the buyer.

To perform these renovations as quickly and efficiently as possible, we have assembled an experienced crew used extensively over the past seven years. Additionally, we have sufficient experience and knowledge to determine the estimated costs and time frame required to complete a project. We anticipate that each project should be completed within 45 days from start to finish.

Based on our experience, the following improvements will significantly increase the value of each property:

1. Update kitchen: Install new cabinets if necessary, ceramic tile floor, new countertops, dishwasher, and other appliances.

2. Replace carpet, refinish wood floors, install new blinds, etc.

3. Update bathroom fixtures, including vanities, etc.

4. Paint interior/exterior as necessary.

5. Perform landscaping to improve exterior appearance.

6. Perform general overall polishing of property. We will keep in mind that our target sale price is $100,000 to $120,000.

Each property will be evaluated on its own merits, but the renovation costs are expected to range between $10,000 and $20,000. Properties that are purchase at $30,000 to $40,000 below market value will provide sufficient differential to achieve our desired return within 90–120 days from acquisition to sale.

Our renovation process model assumes that the six critical tasks stated above represent the entire work to be completed. This assumption will be validated before purchase using a thorough inspection process. Licensed contractors will do our inspections, so there will no surprises regarding the renovation costs.

On occasion, however, a property may be available that may require a much higher remodeling price that would be justified by an opportunity to make a lot of money. These properties may require structural improvements or another major remodeling. These could be properties that are in terrible disrepair.

Another exception to our standard purchase criteria may be a small property surrounded by much larger and more expensive homes in a very desirable neighborhood. These scenarios do not meet our investment strategy but may be considered depending on the project's money.

Selling Properties

After each property has been renovated, it will be listed for sale. As our target consists of 25- to 44-year-olds who may only have enough of a down payment for an FHA mortgage, we expect to offer assistance with closing costs.

Rental Portfolio

Careful attention will be given during the purchase process to find potential rental properties that would meet our long-term investment portfolio criteria. For these properties to meet our standards, they must pass the following performance measures:

1. We must be able to buy and fix the property with minimal cash outlay

2. The property must be located in a desirable area (family-friendly neighborhood) to ensure better than average appreciation and better tenants. It must be purchased at a price below market value.

3. The income and expense streams must be favorable to net a positive cash flow of at least $3,000 per year from each property.

Timeline

In summary, following the timeline identified throughout this document, we expect to purchase an average of one property per month

Managing Our Properties

We are a very successful enterprise with over seven years of investment experience. We have an excellent system in place to continue to monitor our portfolio. We know every month how each property is performing. This is accomplished by our monthly profit and loss statement.

We are confident that our experience and success over the years merit strong consideration to obtain approval for a working line of credit of $100,000.

Thank you very much for your consideration, and we look forward to establishing a mutually beneficial relationship.

COST RECOVERY (DEPRECIATION)

Cost recovery (depreciation) is the periodic allocation of the cost of qualified assets. When a taxpayer, or in some cases a lessee, purchases a qualified asset they are allowed to recover the acquisition cost of the asset through certain deductions set forth in the Internal Revenue Code. The method and length of recovery periods depends on the type of property purchased. Below are the cost recovery tables for the various types of property. These tables are rounded to two decimal points for simplicity. Check with your tax advisor for the actual percentages.

RECOVERY PERCENTAGES FOR RESIDENTIAL RENTAL PROPERTY (27.5 YEARS)

Month Placed in Service

Recovery

Year	Jan	Feb	Mar	Apr	May	June
1	3.48	3.18	2.88	2.58	2.27	1.97
2–27	3.64	3.64	3.64	3.64	3.64	3.64
28	1.88	2.27	2.57	2.87	3.18	3.48
29	0.00	0.00	0.00	0.00	0.00	0.00

Month Placed in Service

Recovery

Year	July	Aug	Sept	Oct	Nov	Dec
1	1.67	1.36	1.06	0.76	0.45	0.15
2–27	3.64	3.64	3.64	3.64	3.64	3.64
28	3.64	3.64	3.64	3.64	3.64	3.64
29	0.15	0.45	0.75	1.06	1.36	1.66

RECOVERY PERCENTAGES FOR NON-RESIDENTIAL RENTAL PROPERTY (39 YEARS)

Month Placed in Service

Recovery

Year	Jan	Feb	Mar	Apr	May	June
1	2.46	2.24	2.05	1.82	1.60	1.39
2–38	2.56	2.56	3.56	2.56	2.56	2.56
39–40 Prorated						

RECOVERY PERCENTAGES FOR NON-RESIDENTIAL RENTAL PROPERTY (39 YEARS)

Month Placed in Service

Recovery

Year	July	Aug	Sept	Oct	Nov	Dec
1	1.18	0.96	0.75	0.53	0.32	0.11
2–38	2.56	2.56	2.56	2.56	2.56	2.56
39–40 Prorated						

RECOVERY PERCENTAGES FOR 15-YEAR LAND IMPROVEMENTS

Recovery Year	Percentage	Recovery Year	Percentage	Recovery Year	Percentage
1	5.00%	6	6.23%	11	5.91%
2	9.50%	7	5.90%	12	5.90%
3	8.55%	8	5.90%	13	5.91%
4	7.70%	9	5.91%	14	5.90%
5	6.93%	10	5.90%	15	5.91%
				16	2.95%

Examples of land improvements that can be depreciated over 15 years are sidewalks, fences, landscaping, and shrubbery.

RECOVERY PERCENTAGES FOR 5-YEAR PERSONAL PROPERTY

Recovery Year	Percentage	Recovery Year	Percentage
1	20.00%	5	11.52%
2	32.00%	6	05.76%
3	19.20%		
4	11.52%		

Examples of personal property that can be depreciated over five years might include a snow blower, lawn mower, carpet, furniture, computer, and so on.

ANALYSIS CASE STUDY FOR RUNNING THE NUMBERS

Case Study: Parker Duplex

Purchase Price	$120,000
Down Payment	$ 24,000
Term	20 years
Interest	6.5%
Closing Costs	$ 3,600
Total Investment	$ 27,600
Income	$850 per side = $20,400
Vacancy	10% ($2040) = $18360
Expenses	
Taxes	$ 2,997
Maintenance	$ 1,800
Insurance	$ 900
Repairs	$ 100
Lawn/Snow Removal	$ 200
Utilities	$ 100
Advertising	$ 50
Supplies	$ 200
Total Expenses	$ (6,347)

FORMULAS FOR RUNNING THE NUMBERS

1. **Gross Scheduled Income:** Total annual income if all units were 100% rented and rent was collected. Represents the highest possible income collection in its current condition.

   Example: $20,400 income potential

2. **Vacancy and Credit Loss:** Income loss due to vacant units or non-payment of rent (credit loss).

   Example: $20,400 × 0.10 = $2,040

3. **Gross Operating Income (GOI):** This is the operating income, less vacancy and credit loss, plus income from other sources such as coin-operated laundry, vending machines, etc.

   Example: $20,400 − $2,040 other = $18,360

4. **Operating Expense (OE):** This are the costs associated with operating the property and includes such things as: property taxes, maintenance, insurance, repairs, lawn/snow removal, utilities, advertising, supplies, trash removal, property management, etc.

   Does not include debt service, income taxes or depreciation.

   Example: $6,347

5. **Net Operating Income (NOI):** Is one of the most import-
    ant measures because it is used to determine the return on
    the purchase price of the property. an objective measure of
    a property's income stream. It is the gross operating in-
    come, less the operating expenses. It is simply the annual *in-
    come* generated by the property *operations*, and deducting
    all expenses incurred.

    Example: $18,360 – $6,347 = $12,013

    Note: Do not include debt service or capital expenses in NOI.

    Capital Expenditures are basically "one-time" costs that are
    not included in the operations of the property. Things like new
    windows, roof, driveway etc. By including capital expenditures
    in the operating expenses, it will lower the NOI, therefore low-
    ering the value.

    Additionally, NOI can be used to as a strategy to increase
    value. As an example, increasing the rent and decreasing the ex-
    penses where possible.

6. **Cash Flow Before Taxes (CFBT):** Is net operating income,
    less debt service and capital expenditures, plus earned
    interest.

    It represents the annual cash available before the consider-
    ation of income taxes. Cash flow is the flow of money the prop-
    erty generates, (in and out). It represents the money, without
    regard to the deductions for tax purposes. While a tax return
    may show a loss, the actual cash flow of the property may show
    profits, or vice versa.

Formula:

Net Operating Income NOI – Debt Service

– Capital Improvements

+ Loan Proceeds for loans to finance operations (if any)

+ Interest earned (if any)

= Cash Flow Before Taxes

Example: $12,013 – $8,589 = $3,424

7. **Taxable Income or Loss:** This is the net operating income, less interest, real property and capital additional, depreciation, loan points and closing costs, plus interest earned on property bank accounts.

    Taxable income may be negative as well as a positive. If it is negative, it can shelter other earnings and result in a negative tax liability.

    Formula:

    Net Operating Income – Interest Paid

    – Depreciation – Amortization + Interest Earned

    = Taxable Income or Loss

    Example: 12,013 – 6,169 – 3,735 = $2,109

8. **Tax Liability:** This is what one pays or saves in taxes.

    Formula:

    Taxable income or loss multiplied by investor tax bracket

    Example: $2,109 × 0.28 = $590

9. **Cash Flow After Taxes (CFAT):** This is the amount of cash generated from the property after consideration for taxes that can be spent as the investors wants.

It is the bottom line and is calculated by subtracting the tax liability from cash flow before taxes. It is the measure that determines the ability of the property to generate cash flow through its operations.

   Formula:

   Cash Flow Before Taxes – Tax Liability

   Example: $3,424 – $590 = $2834

10. **Gross Rent Multiplier (GRM):** This provides a simple method you can use to estimate the market value of any income property. It is the ratio of the price of the property to its annual rental income before expenses such as property taxes, insurance, utilities, maintenance (see operating expenses).

    Formula:

    Price / Potential Gross Income = GRM

    Example:

    $120,000 / $20,400 = 5.88%

11. **Capitalization Rate:** Cap rate (as it is more commonly called) is the rate at which you discount future income to determine its present value. Capitalization rate is used to estimate the potential return of the investment. This is done by dividing the net operating income by the proposed asking price. The higher the CAP rate the better for the buyer (lower purchase price). The lower the CAP rate the better for the seller (higher asking price)

Formula:

NOI / Value = Cap Rate

Example: $12,013 / $120,000 = 10.01%

NOI/Cap Rate = Value

Example: $12,001 / 8.21% = $120,012

Formula:

Value × Cap rate= NOI

Example: $120,000 × 10.01% = $12,013

12. **Cash on Cash Return (COC):** This represents the ratio between the property's annual cash flow (usually the first year before taxes) and the amount of the initial capital investment (down payment, loan fees, and acquisition costs). It is a very important ratio to evaluate the long-term performance of a property investment. You can compare the (COC) to a return of a certificate of deposit that as an example pays annual return, of 4.5%. The 4.5% is the Cash on Cash ratio.

Formula:

Cash Flow Before Taxes CFBT/Cash Invested = Cash on Cash

Example: $3,424 / $27,600 = 12.41%

13. **Operating Expense Ratio (OER):** This provides the ratio for the property's total operating expenses to its gross operating income (GOI). The operating expense ratio is a useful tool when comparing the expenses of similar properties.

If a piece of property has a much higher OER for an expense, such as maintenance, an investor should see that as a red flag and should look deeper into why maintenance expenses are so much higher than comparable properties. For example, the maintenance expenses are $1800/$18,360 = 9.8% of overall operating expenses of 34.57%.

Formula:

Operating Expenses / GOI = Operating Expense Ratio

Example: $6347 / $18,360 = 34.57%

14. **Debt Coverage Ratio (DCR) and known as Debt Service Coverage Ratio (DSCR):** This is the ratio between the property's net operating income and annual debt service for the year. A DCR of 1 indicates that the income is just sufficient to cover debt service payments (not good) A DCR of less than 1 indicates the property is unable to generate income sufficient enough to cover its payments.

A property with a DCR of 1.25 generates 1.25 times as much annual income as the annual debt service on the property. In this example, the property produces 25%.

The greater the DCR is above 1.2 the preferable it is by lenders because it represents the property generates more than enough income to repay the debt service. The higher the DCR the better. Lenders typically require a DCR of 1.2 or more.

Factors that can affect these ratios may be such things as: interest rate, down payment, vacancy rates in the area, over supply of properties, current economic outlook, overall demand for real estate, physical condition and location of the property, age, crime in the area, proximity to shopping, schools, property management, overall upkeep etc.

On another note, lenders are now starting to use what is called global (DCR). This is a ratio that combines properties with weak cash flow, or a property with a lower CAP rate, to still be able to qualify for a commercial loan.

Formula:

Net Operating Income/Annual Debt Service = Debt Coverage Ratio

Example: $12,013 / $ 8,589 = 1.399%

15. **The Break-Even Ratio (BER):** It measures the portion of money going out against money coming in and tells the investor what part of gross operating income will be used by all estimated expenses.

    Lenders use the break-even ratio as one of their analysis methods when considering getting a loan. Too high of a break-even ratio is a red flag. The BER tells the lender how vulnerable a property might be to default on its debt in the event the rental income should decline.

    The result always must be less than 100% for an investment to be viable (the lower, the better). Lenders typically require a BER of 85% or less

    Formula:

    Operating Expenses + Debt Service/Gross Operating Income = BER

    Example: ($6,347 + $8,589) / $18,360 = 81.35%

16. Loan to Value (LTV): This is the ratio of the loan amount to the appraised value of the property. It measures the percent of the property's appraised value or selling price.

A higher LTV means greater leverage (higher financial risk). A lower LTV means less leverage (lower financial risk) for the lender.

Formula:

Loan Amount/Less of Appraised Value or Selling Price
= LTV

17. Return on Investment with Appreciation: ROI with Appreciation.

Formula:

(Cash Flow Before Taxes (CFBT)+Principal Reduction–
Taxes Paid)

+ Appreciation Estimate / Cash Invested

Example: ($3,424 + $2,420 – 590 + $2,400 / $27,600 = 27.73%

18. Return on Investment without Appreciation: ROI w/o Appreciation. It considers 3 of the 4 benefits-Income, Principal Reduction, and Depreciation. This will let you know how the investment compares against other properties in consideration.

Formula:

Cash Flow Before Taxes + Principal Reduction

– Taxes Paid / Cash Invested

Example: ($3424 + $2,420 – $590 / $27,600 = 19.03%

19. **Annual Debt Service (ADS):** Total paid on loan for the year. The total amount paid in interest payments and principal for one year. The total principal and interest paid on loan for one year. This is a good way to calculate the debt service a lender requires as a minimum with a DCR of 1.25.

Formula:

ADS = NOI/DCR

Examples:

$12,013 / 1.399 = $8,589

$12,013 / 1.25 = $9610

> **Bottom line:** The above formulas should guide the investor to make decisions based on desired goals. Each investor has different goals and objectives, so what may be good for one will not be good for another.

PROPERTY ANALYSIS BUY AND HOLD INSTRUCTIONS

Note: Only change highlighted categories on the form:

1. Property address: number of units

2. Purchase cost: (purchase price, down payment, and closing costs.

3. Financing: (term, interest rate, same for the second mortgage.

4. Depreciation: Refer to depreciation schedule. Analysis intended to be for year one only. It is difficult to predict more than the first year.

    a. Land value - Use County Assessor values (Can't depreciate land)

    b. Personal property (If appliances such as stove, refrigerator, dishwasher, washer, dryer, etc., are included in the purchase, estimate a value for each).

    c. Land improvement (such things as fencing, landscaping, sidewalks, driveways, etc.)

    d. Building value is the difference of a, b, c and should add up to the purchase price. a $22,600, b $2000, c $1000, building value $$94,400.

5. Annual rent: Use vacancy at 10%.

6. Annual expenses: Change and or add categories as needed- For this purpose, you can include other expenses in misc.

7. Annual debt service: Interest is only for year 1. (Use any amortization schedule.

8. Net operating income: Tax bracket can be changed as needed. Ask the client for their tax bracket from the previous year or estimate 28%?

9. Appreciation estimate. (When estimating it is better to be on the low side even though appreciation has been higher (3-4%) for the past couple of years)

The Analysis form is for informational purposes only. Be sure to ask your attorney or CPA for advice.

Notes:

_____

_____

_____

PROPERTY ANALYSIS BUY AND HOLD (BLANK)

Property Analysis Buy and Hold

I.	Gross Operating Income		$_____	
	minus	Operating Expenses	$_____	
	equals	Net Operating Income	$_____	
	minus	annual debt service	$_____	
	equals	Cash Flow Before Taxes	$_____	
II.	7) Annual Debt Service		$_____	
	minus	Interest	$ 6,169	
	equals	Principal reduction (PR)	$_____	$
III.	8) Net Operating Income		$_____	
	minus	Interest	$_____	
	minus	Total Depreciation	$_____	
	equals	Taxable Income	$_____	
	times (8)	tax bracket	_____%	
	equals	Taxes paid (TP)	$_____	
IV.	9) Appreciation Estimate (AE)		$_____	$_____
V.	ROI with Appr.(CFBT+PR-TP+AE/cash inv.		_____%	
VI.	ROI without Appr.(CFBT+PR-TP/ cash inv.		_____%	
VII.	Capitalization Rate(NOI divided by purchase price)		_____%	
VIII.	Cash on cash(cash flow bef. taxes div.by cash inv)		_____%	
IX.	Gross Rent Multiplier(sale price div.by annual rent)		_____%	
X.	Debt Coverage Ratio(NOI div. by debt service)		_____%	
XI.	Operating Exp.Ratio(op.exp. div. by gross op.inc.)		_____%	
XII.	Break Even Ratio(BER)= Op. Exp.+ Debt Service/Gross Op. Inc.		_____%	
XIII.	Cash Flow After Taxes CFAT (CFAT)=CFBT-Taxes paid		$_____	

This form is designed to assist in estimating the first-year benefits of a real estate investment. It does not consider the effects of selling or exchanging the property in the future. This form is not a substitute for legal advice. Anyone contemplating the purchase of a real estate investment should seek the advice of competent legal and tax advisors.

PROPERTY ANALYSIS BUY AND HOLD (SAMPLE)

Property Analysis Buy and Hold					
1) Property Address	Parker Duplex		No. of Units		2
2) Purchase Cost	120,000.00				
Down Payment	24,000.00				
Closing Costs	3,600.00				
Total Investment	27,600				
	TERM	AMOUNT	RATE		P & I
3) FINANCING 1st Mortgage	20	$96,000.00	6.50%	$	715.75
FINANCING 2nd Mortgage	10		7.50%	$	-
4) Depreciation				Year 1	
Land Value		0.00%	$ 22,600.00	$	22,600.00
Personal Property		20.00%	$ 2,000.00	$	400.00
Building Value		3.48%	$ 94,400.00	$	3,285
Land Improvement Value		5.00%	$ 1,000.00	$	50.00
Total Depreciation			$ 120,000.00	$	3,735
5) Annual Rent		$ 20,400			
Less Vacancy Rate (10%)		$ 2,040			
Other Income					
Gross Operating Income		$ 18,360			
6) Annual Operating Expenses					
Real Estate Taxes	$ 2,997.00				
Maintenance	$ 1,800.00				
Insurance	$ 900.00				
repairs	$ 100.00				
Management					
Misc.					
Lawn and snow	$ 200.00				
Utilities	$ 100.00				
Advertising	$ 50.00				
supplies	$ 200.00				
TOTAL	$ 6,347				

Gross Operating Income		$	18,360	
minus	Operating Expenses	$	6,347	
equals	Net Operating Income	$	12,013	
minus	annual debt service	$	8,589	
equals	Cash Flow Before Taxes (C.F.B.T.)	$	3,424	
7) Annual Debt Service		$	8,589	
minus	Interest		$6,169	
equals	Principal reduction(PR)	$	2,420	$ (93,580)
8) Net Operating Income (N.O.I.)		$	12,013	
minus	Interest	$	6,169	
minus	Total Depreciation	$	3,735	
equals	Taxable Income	$	2,109	
times tax bracket	tax bracket		28%	
equals	Taxes paid (TP)	$	591	
9) Appreciation Estimate (AE)			2.00%	$ 2,400
10)ROI with Appr.(CFBT+PR-TP+AE/cash inv.			27.73%	
11)ROI without Appr.(CFBT+PR-TP/ cash inv.			19.04%	
12)Capitalization Rate(NOI divided by purchase price)			10.01%	
13)Cash on cash(cash flow bef. taxes div.by cash inv)			12.41%	
14)Gross Rent Multiplier(sale price div.by annual rent)			5.88%	
15)Debt Coverage Ratio(NOI div. by debt service)			1.399	
16)Operating Exp.Ratio(op.exp. div. by gross op.inc.)			34.57%	
17)Break Even Ratio(BER)= Op. Exp.+ Debt Service/Gross Op.			81.35%	
18)Cash Flow After Taxes (CFAT)= CFBT-Taxes Paid		$	2,833	

This form is designed to assist in estimating the first-year benefits of a real estate investment. It does
not consider the effects of selling or exchanging the property in the future. This form is not a substitute
for legal advice. Anyone contemplating the purchase of a real estate investment should seek the advice
of competent legal and tax advisors.   4/30/2021

SAMPLE INTERVIEW QUESTIONS TO ASK TENANTS OVER THE PHONE

Question 1: *Why are you moving?*

This question can tell you a lot about the tenant. Listen for legitimate reasons for moving, such as a job change or wanting more room. Look for red flags such as being evicted, complaining about their landlord, and so on.

Question 2: *What is your move-in date?*

If the tenant wants to move in tomorrow, they may not be the most responsible person. Most landlords require 30 days' notice to terminate a lease, and if this tenant wants to move in tomorrow, something may be off. Special circumstances do apply, such as a pay cut, a sudden job transfer, or domestic abuse. Still, responsible tenants usually will start their search for an apartment at least a month before their anticipated move-in date.

Question 3: *What is your monthly income?*

This question can help you determine whether the prospective tenant can afford the property. Most renters spend between 30 and 35 percent of their income on rent and utilities. Keep in mind that the monthly income may not tell the whole story. Additional factors such as how much debt they have, will impact their ability to pay on time. The amount of debt can be discovered by running a credit check.

Question 4: *Can you pay the security deposit and the first month's rent before you move in?*

A prospect who does not have a full deposit will likely have ongoing financial problems. You do not want to start a tenant relationship with the tenant already owing you money. You should never allow a tenant to move in without paying the security deposit and rent. Do not negotiate or make exceptions to this rule.

Question 5: How many people will be living in the property?

If there are only two bedrooms and the family has two or three kids, the property is probably too small. Keep in mind that the greater the number of people who live in a property, the more wear and tear they will create. If the property has a finished basement that does not have an egress window, make sure you stipulate that no one can sleep in the basement under any circumstances. You do not want any potential legal issues.

Question 6: Do you have any references I can contact, such as your current and former landlord?

If the prospective tenant hesitates or makes excuses for not providing references, they are probably hiding something. References from an employer or current pay stubs for the last two pay periods may also work.

It is important to contact current and former landlords. Their current landlord may not tell you the whole truth because they may just be trying to get rid of the tenant.

Question 7: Is there anything I need to know about you as I run credit and background checks?

If they tell you upfront that they did something stupid as a young adult, it may not be a deal-breaker. If they have not had any issues recently and have steady employment, use your gut to decide. You must have the prospective tenant sign a form giving their permission to run credit and background checks. Verbal consent is not binding.

Question 8: Have you ever been evicted?

While the prospective tenant may not tell the truth, this question is still worth asking. Directly asking the prospective tenant if they have been evicted will allow the tenant to explain the situation. Reasonable people can fall on hard times, and the eviction may have happened several years back. If the eviction happened before the two landlord verifications, you may want to use your discretion. If the eviction was for causing damage or excessive noise, these behaviors may not have changed.

Question 9: Do you have any pets?

If you have a "no pets" policy, a prospective tenant with a pet will be a deal-breaker. If your policy allows pets, it is essential to find out what kind of pet it is, and you want to see it. If it is a pit bull or Rottweiler, makes sure you check with your insurance company to see if your policy covers you if the dog bites some-one. Regardless, make sure they have liability insurance and that you are also an assignee. The current trend is to charge pet rent instead of a pet deposit. The pet rent can be $25 and up per pet. (A deposit is not considered income, but pet rent is.)

Question 10: Do you have any questions?

This will give the tenant a chance to ask questions about your property, the screening process, or anything else that comes to mind. This is important because even if the tenant has answered all of the questions to your liking, the tenant must also want to live in your property.

LEASE AGREEMENT (SAMPLE)

THIS IS A LEGALLY AND BINDING CONTRACT. IF YOU DO NOT UNDERSTAND PLEASE CONSULT AN ATTORNEY

THIS AGREEMENT made by and between _____(hereafter called OWNER), and _____ (herein called TENANT(s) and agrees to rent _____. for one year beginning on _____. Resident agrees to pay a monthly rental of $ _____ per month on or before the 1st day of each month and considered to be late after that date.
RENT SHALL BE PAID BY CHECK, MONEY ORDER, CERTIFIED CHECK, CASHIERS CHECK. Rent payment can be DIRECT DEPOSITED AT ANY SECURITY NATIONAL BANK Branch. If sending rent payment by mail send to IDNAR Properties LLC, PO Box 242, Boys Town, NE 68010.Tenant responsible for $_____ equal payments of $_____ per month.

This agreement is subject to the following:

1. ____ **LEASE RENEWAL.** This lease agreement is not constructed to be automatically renewed at the end of the term for which drawn, however the intent to renew this agreement by the Tenant(s) will be assumed. All parties will need to sign a new agreement in order to activate a renewal term. If Tenant(s) intends to vacate the Premises at the end of the lease term, Tenant(s) must give at least sixty (60) days written notice prior to the end of this lease if they intend to renew the lease or vacate. This lease does not automatically renew without the approval of owner. In the event tenant does not to want to sign another yearly lease (if approved by owner) then it is understood that Tenant will rent the property on a month to month to basis for an additional $100 per month for a total of $___

2. _____. **LATE PAYMENT CHARGE**: Resident shall be charged **ten (10%)** of the monthly rent balance plus any applicable administrative charges, which shall be automatically added to the above rental payment if the OWNER/AGENT does not receive the rent by the 4th day after the due date. Payment of said late charge shall not waive OWNER/AGENT's right to terminate this rental agreement following non-payment of the rent as hereafter provided. The Resident will be charged forty ($40.00) dollars for any check returned by the Resident's bank unpaid. Such check charge shall be automatically added to the balance of the Resident's account due to OWNER/AGENT and shall be in addition to any rent or late charge then owning. Returned checks shall be redeemed only with money orders, certified, or cashier's check. OWNER/AGENT shall then have the right to refuse all personal checks tendered as payment after that. **The Resident will be responsible for all costs incurred to collect money owed to OWNER/AGENT. If the eviction process has begun against the Resident, a $275.00 lease reinstatement fee shall be applied to stop the eviction process. If Resident's first full month's rent is late, Owner shall have the right to terminate AGREEMENT.**

   _____**It is agreed any payments received by Resident or on behalf of Resident shall be applied first to late fees, then to maintenance expenses, any damages identified before Resident moves out, and any other services provided by OWNER/AGENT, then to rent.**

   _____**Resident shall be afforded (1) free Three-Day Notice administrative fee. Resident shall be assessed a $25 administrative fee for each subsequent Three-Day Notice for the remaining duration of the Lease Agreement at the option of Owner/Agent.**

   _____**Residents understand that they nor their guests ARE NOT permitted to smoke inside the unit.**

3. _____**ENTRY**: OWNER/AGENT shall have a master key to all locks. RESIDENT SHALL NOT INSTALL AUXILIARY LOCK OR RE-KEY EXISTING LOCKS. OWNER/AGENT may enter the unit without consent or notice in case of emergency. The Resident hereby consents to allow OWNER/AGENT to enter the unit for inspection, make repairs or alterations, or exhibit to prospective Residents, purchasers, mortgagee, appraisers, or insurance agents upon notice, verbal written OR by any method, given within 24-hour notice before entry is made.

4. _____**UTILITIES**: OWNER/AGENT shall pay for and furnish the following utilities if indicated by OWNER/AGENT next to the utility service below; 'RESIDENT' indicates that the RESIDENT is responsible for the cost. RESIDENT agrees they will pay the difference in the ELECTRIC bill if the monthly bill is greater than 10% of the monthly rent. RESIDENT agrees they will pay the difference in the GAS bill if the amount owed is greater than 10% of the monthly rent.

  1. OPPD-Resident (Electricity)   **2. MUD** (Gas, water, sewer)
  RESIDENT has one day from lease signing to procure and put utilities in RESIDENT's name, or OWNER/AGENT has the right after this date to shut them off without further notice to RESIDENT. RESIDENT agrees to pay an administrative fee of $20 per day, per utility if any of the utilities are not in Resident's name. RESIDENT must keep utilities on and if RESIDENT does not, OWNER/AGENT may evict the RESIDENT or at the option of OWNER/AGENT put utilities in his name and evict RESIDENT. In the event RESIDENT contacts any utility provider and requests the discontinuation of said utility, then RESIDENT agrees this shall be considered an act of abandonment of the premises and OWNER/AGENT shall be entitled upon receiving verification from any utility provider that RESIDENT has requested the utilities to be terminated, to take possession of the property without further action by OWNER/AGENT or RESIDENT.

5. _____**NON-COMPLIANCE BY RESIDENT**: If Resident doesn't comply with any term of this rental agreement or with any rules and regulations now in effect or any rules and regulations, OWNER/AGENT may institute in the future with notice to Resident, then OWNER/AGENT may give written notice to Resident specifying acts or omissions constituting breach, and rental agreement will terminate on a date not less than 30 days after receipt of notice if breach is not remedied within 14 days and rental agreement will then terminate as provided in such notice. OWNER/AGENT MAY TERMINATE THIS RENTAL AGREEMENT IF RENT IS UNPAID WHEN DUE AND RESIDENT FAILS TO PAY RENT WITH THREE (3) DAYS AFTER WRITTEN NOTICE BY OWNER/AGENT OF NON-PAYMENT AND HIS INTENTION TO TERMINATE THE RENTAL AGREEMENT IF RENT IS NOT PAID WITHIN SAID THREE DAYS. Resident shall always provide to OWNER/AGENT an active phone number where Resident may be contacted.

6. _____**DAMAGES**: OWNER/AGENT IS NOT LIABLE FOR AND DOES NOT PROVIDE INSURANCE ON RESIDENTS PERSONAL PROPERTY, whether in the unit, in storage areas or anywhere on the premises and OWNER/AGENT shall not be responsible for theft, damage or loss to any property of the Resident, whether or not caused by OWNER/AGENT negligence. Each party waives all claims for recovery from the other for loss or damage of any property insured under collective insurance policies of insurance. The Resident will give notice to OWNER/AGENT of any breakage, damage, waste or litter or of any structure, unit or appliances or common area, and if caused by Resident, his family or guest, or by failure to promptly report same. Resident shall reimburse OWNER/AGENT for the total cost of repairs, waste, damage or litter and replacement cost of all property damaged, to be paid as additional rent, and to be due and payable on next rental date after demand by OWNER/AGENT.

7. _____**BROKEN WINDOWS, DOORS OR SCREENS**: RESIDENT shall pay for broken windows, torn or missing screens or storms, or broken doors unless RESIDENT send OWNER/AGENT a list in writing enumerating torn screens, broken windows and missing inserts within ten days of execution of the lease.

8. _____**VANDALISM**: RESIDENT is responsible for all vandalism committed to the inside of the property since the property is in the control of the RESIDENT. **ADHESIVE STICKERS**: RESIDENT is liable for the cost of removing all adhesive stickers to doors, walls, and windows.

9. _____**ASSIGNMENT AND OCCUPANCY OF PREMISES**: Resident shall not assign or sublet said premises without written consent of OWNER/AGENT. This rental agreement shall always be subordinate to any mortgage or deed of trust, which may now or hereafter affect the premises and no further instrument shall be needed to affect this subordination. The only individuals allowed to reside in residence are those above-mentioned RESIDENTS, and the following individual's N/A There shall be one-half of one month rent as a re-leasing fee.

   _____**USE AND OCCUPANCY OF PREMISES**: Resident shall use dwelling unit only for private dwelling with occupancy limited to those adults mentioned above and in compliance with the *Building Officials Code Administrators* International BOCA code occupancy standards. Residents shall not permit the use of said premises for any unlawful, immoral, or objectionable purposes or anything that may create a fire hazard. The resident will comply with all applicable governmental laws and regulations. Resident SHALL notify OWNER/AGENT in writing of any individual that occupies this residence for longer than seven days. OWNER/AGENT SHALL assess a $200.00 per month, per Resident fee for ANY unauthorized people

10. _____**RESIDENT is aware that drug trafficking is a violation of the law; and that illegal drug trafficking or use is a substantial breach of these lease terms, subjecting Resident to immediate termination of the lease.**

11. _____**DUTIES of RESIDENT**: The Resident agrees to:
    a. Maintain premises in clean and safe condition and upon lease termination put premises in as clean a condition except for ordinary wear and tear as when occupancy commenced.
    b. Dispose of dwelling unit all ashes, rubbish, garbage and other waste in a clean and safe manner and plastic garbage bags; keep all plumbing fixtures as clean as condition permits, use in a reasonable manner all electrical, plumbing, heating, air-conditioning and other facilities and appliances. TRASH And GARBAGE SHALL BE KEPT IN PLASTIC BAGS AND REMOVED TO OUTSIDE TRASH CANS OR DUMPSTERS, AS PROVIDED.
    c. Resident acknowledges that all drains in the rented unit are free running and that any stoppages of the sink, rub or toilet drains within the unit will be caused by Resident. Resident agrees to pay the cost necessary to clear any such drain stoppages. This provision does not address main line or joint use drain lines that shall remain the responsibility of the OWNER/AGENT. RESIDENT AGREES TO PURCHASE AND USE A DRAIN PLUNGER, AND TO NOT USE ANY LIQUID DRAIN OPENERS, BEFORE CALLING OWNER/AGENT TO CLEAR DRAIN STOPPAGES. Resident agrees to pay for any rain cleaning caused by the Residents negligence.
    d. Not deface, damage, waste, litter or remove any part of the premises or permit any persons or guest to do so; conduct himself/herself and guest in a manner not to disturb neighbor's peaceful enjoyment of the premises.
    e. Abide by the existing rules and regulations attached hereto and make a part of this agreement and any further rules and regulations adopted hereafter following notice by OWNER/AGENT to Resident.
    f. Obtain OWNER/AGENT's prior written permission before making any alterations, additions, improvements, including painting or changes in the premises, whether exterior or interior. Any alterations, additions, improvements or changes that the OWNER/AGENT does permit shall become the property of the OWNER/AGENT and shall remain on the premises at the termination of the Resident's tenancy.

g. Give notice to the OWNER/AGENT of any anticipated extended absence more than seven (7) days. Said notice must be given no later than the first day of the extended absence. If the Resident abandons the dwelling unit, the OWNER/AGENT shall take immediate possession. The total absence from the premises without notice to the OWNER/AGENT for seven (7) days shall constitute abandonment.

h. Resident SHALL provide access to the unit at the convenience of the Owner/Agent once Resident authorizes/requests service to the unit.

i. Residents and or guests shall not engage in ANY illegal or illicit activity while occupying the premises.

j. Resident shall keep unit free from all bug infestation.

k. Furnace filters if you have access to the furnace it is the Resident's responsibility to change the furnace filter monthly. Under no circumstances the thermostat in the winter should not be set below 60 degrees. If you will be away for an extended period in the winter, make sure someone checks the property to make sure the furnace is working properly. If negligence is proven damages will be the tenant responsibility

l. **Any damage to the premises shall charge the repair rates as posted as expressed in this Agreement and its attachments.**

12. ____**APPLIANCES AND FURNISHINGS**: Resident acknowledges that any stove, refrigerator, dishwasher, carpet, garbage disposal, drapes/blinds, or any other appliances or personal property now in said unit shall remain in the property of the OWNER/AGENT and Resident shall not damage, alter or remove same. Any improvements made by Resident shall become the property of the OWNER/AGENT. In the Event of any service call or repair to garbage disposal, toilet or other plumbing necessitated by act or omission of Resident, then in such event, Resident shall reimburse OWNER/AGENT for the cost thereof to be paid as additional rent due and payable on the next rental date after demand by OWNER/AGENT. Appliances includes are as follows:
X Refrigerator   X Central AC   X Stove/range   __ Window air units
-- Dishwasher   __Washer   ___Dryer

13. **X_ PETS**: PERMITTED. (Check applicable provision below)
Pet Description: _____
Also, $ N/A Additional rent per month shall be assessed for pet rent (Included in rent). DAMAGES MAY NOT BE LIMITED TO THIS FEE AND MAY BE OFFSET AGAINST THE RESIDENT'S SECURITY DEPOSIT MADE HEREUNDER. Pet is specifically limited to and is to be controlled so as not to disturb the peaceful enjoyment of the Residents or to be destructive to premises or common area. Pets cannot be of a dangerous breed. Any breach of this provision is deemed non-compliance allowing termination of rental agreement by OWNER/AGENT.
The Resident is also to comply with local municipal pet regulations. Without prior written authorization Resident shall not be permitted to keep a pet at the residence for any reason.
____**IN THE EVENT RESIDENT HAS NOT RECEIVED WRITTEN AUTHORIZATION FROM LANDLORD AND IS FOUND TO HAVE ADDITIONAL PETS, THERE SHALL BE A $200- PER MONTH PET RENT ASSESSMENT FOR EACH PET.**

14. ____**CONDITION OF PREMISES:** Resident accepts premises in present condition, Resident shall surrender premises at the termination of the rental agreement in as good and rentable condition as received, except reasonable wear and tear.
____**RESIDENT ACCEPTS UNIT IN AS-IS CONDITION**

15. ____PROVISIONS: Resident to give 30 days written notice of intent to vacate the premises after the lease has been fulfilled or Security Deposit made hereunder SHALL not be refunded. Rent shall continue until keys are returned to OWNER/AGENT. Additionally: **Resident shall be responsible for snow/ice removal and lawn care except for areas common to other Residents at the leased premises. RESIDENT SHALL PLACE TRASH/GARBAGE INTO PROPER CONTAINERS. RESIDENT SHALL PUT ALL TRASH/GARBAGE IN SEALED CLEAR PLASTIC BAGS.** In the event, there is an eviction, judgment, and writ issued Resident shall be required to pay a Lease Reinstatement Fee of $275.00.

16. ___SECURITY DEPOSIT: Resident shall pay herewith a Security Deposit of $ ____. This SECURITY DEPSOSIT IS NOT A RENTAL PAYMENT.

17. ____TERMS FOR SECURITY DEPOSIT REFUND
   a. Entire residence; including range, refrigerator, bathroom, fixtures, closets, and cabinets are clean. Refrigerator shall be defrosted
   b. No indentations or scratches in the woodwork
   c. Floor shall be restored to original condition
   d. If Resident has installed wall-to-wall carpeting or otherwise affixed carpeting to the floor, carpeting shall remain. Any window shades, curtain rods, drapery hardware or other items affixed to premises shall remain with the unit.
   e. Resident shall have paid all delinquent rent or other charges made under this rental agreement
   f. Resident shall cooperate in allowing premises to be shown to prospective Residents during the last 30 days of occupancy
   g. All debris, rubbish, and discards shall have been removed from premises by Resident and placed in proper containers. All keys shall have been returned. Resident shall have left forwarding address with the OWNER/AGENT
   h. Resident shall have complied with pet provision as stipulated above
   i. Full term of rental agreement has expired, and all provisions comply with including notice of termination
   j. No damage to premises or contents thereof or common area beyond normal wear and tear
   k. The OWNER/AGENT and only the OWNER/AGENT will determine whether the premises will qualify as "clean".

18. ___COLLECTION COST: Resident shall be responsible for all costs of collection for unpaid rents, late fees, uncollectible checks and maintenance or repair charges for damage or rubbish removal caused by Resident or Resident's guests. Such cost will be added to the Resident's rental account and a service charge of 1.5% per month from the date incurred will be charged on all unpaid amounts as well as any collection costs or fees.

19. ___RESIDENT SHALL BE RESPONSIBLE for returning the dwelling unit in a clean and undamaged condition, subject only to normal wear and tear. Resident hereby agrees that any personal property left on the premises after the keys are returned to the OWNER/AGENT shall be considered abandoned and hereby grants permission to the OWNER/AGENT to have such property disposed of in any manner deemed appropriate by the OWNER/AGENT, without further notice, and any cost of removal shall be the obligation of the Resident.

20. Any promotional monetary credit given as an inducement to enter this Agreement shall be rescinded, and Resident shall be obligated to reimburse Owner an amount equal to said inducement in the event the Resident does not complete the entire term of this Agreement. A $25 check processing fee shall be applied if during lease term Resident requests, a refund of a credit balance that may exist.

21. ___ RESIDENT acknowledges there are operating smoke/fire detectors in each bedroom as well in each floor. Additionally, there is 1 Carbon monoxide detector in each living floor (check if applicable ___Basement, ___ First Floor __ Second Floor). Upon possession, Resident shall immediately test all smoke detectors and notify OWNER/AGENT IF NOT FUNCTIONAL. It is the responsibility of RESIDENT to test detectors on a regular basis and change batteries as needed.

22. ____Move out Inspection of the premises will be made only after Resident has moved out completely and SURRENDERED KEYS. Request for the return of Security Deposit must be made in writing to IDNAR Properties LLC –PO Box 242 Boys Town NE, 68010. Security Deposit will be refunded within 14 days of a request by check mailed to the forwarding address **AS REQUIRED BY THE NEBRASKA LANDLORD'S AND TENANT'S ACT.**

23.____ **Security Deposit will not be hand delivered. RESIDENT AGREES TO PAY THE LAST MONTH'S RENT IN FULL AND ACKNOWLEDGES THAT SECURITY DEPOSIT IS NOT TO BE USED AS A RENTAL PAYMENT. The security deposit shall be delivered to the primary account holder.** Any language contained in this agreement that pertains to any gender shall be deemed to be neutral and apply to both genders equally.

24.____**SPECIAL PROVISIONS**. Resident agrees to provide Owner a copy of a Renter's insurance policy. Otherwise, Resident understands an additional $25 monthly fee may be assessed. without a policy

25._____.**RESIDENT** may buy out an executed Lease Agreement only if:
- Residents account is current at the time of notification
- With the delivery of 3 months future rent in the form of certified funds.

26. _____This agreement is not binding until signed by OWNER or OWNER's agent. ALL RESIDENTS SIGNING ARE JOINTLY AND SEVERALLY LIABLE. The owner shall have the right to place a For SALE sign and lock box on the premises and Tenant will cooperate if a minimum of 24-hour notice is given.

27._____**RESIDENT** responsible for all ice and snow removal and accepts full responsibility and hold owner harmless for all liability for damages, injuries or claims resulting to promptly from Tenant's negligence in failing to promptly remove snow and ice.

28._____**RESIDENT** shall keep the lawn mowed on a regular basis and trim all bushes as needed along the foundation, and any fence lines. If Tenant's fails to mow the premises for three weeks in succession, Owner is authorized to hire someone to mow the premises and charge a minimum of $50 for same. If bushes, volunteer trees etc. are allowed to grow by Tenant, Tenant agrees to pay a minimum charge of $100 for this service.

29._____. **FURNACE/AIR. RESIDENT** shall change the furnace filters monthly during the winter and if central air conditioner every month during the summer. If property has central air, Tenant shall hose off the outside compressor and keep it free of tree lint, weeds, grass, and any other debris. Tenant will be charged for service call and any repairs required due to failure to change the filters or keep outside compressor clean.) During winter months the thermostat should not be set lower than 60 degrees. In the event you will be away for a few days it's imperative that someone checks the property to make sure the furnace is functioning properly. If it is determined that Tenant was negligent any damages will be incurred by Tenant

30._____**SNOW REMOVAL**. Resident is responsible for snow removal of driveway, steps, sidewalks within 24 hours after snow stops and Resident will be liable should anyone be hurt because of negligence.

31.__N/A___ Under no circumstances is anyone allowed to use the basement as a bedroom.

Tenant Name:
Signature _____ Date _____

Phone _____ Email address_____

Signature _____Date _____

Phone _____ Email address _____

Owner
Signature _____ Date _____

Phone _____Email address _____

TENANT SCREENING QUESTIONS THAT ARE OFF-LIMITS

(Source: The balance.com)

Landlords have a right to screen prospective tenants, and you'll want to be as thorough as possible. Certain questions are simply off-limits. Asking a tenant about their race or religion are big no-nos, as are questions about arrest records.

There are some main topics you'll want to steer clear of if you're going to stay on the right side of the law.

QUESTIONS THAT VIOLATE FAIR HOUSING LAWS

Avoid any question that could seem discriminatory toward a certain class of people. This can be interpreted as discrimination under the Federal Fair Housing Law or under your state's Fair Housing Law.

The Federal Fair Housing Act protects seven classes: race, color, religion, sex, national origin, disability, and familial status. In addition, many states have additional protected classes such as marital status and sexual orientation. Here are a few questions or comments you'll want to avoid, even if you're just throwing them out there to make innocent conversation:

- You would love the area. A lot of minorities live here.
- Are you white or Hispanic?
- There aren't a lot of temples around here, so I don't know if you'd fit in.
- I don't feel safe renting to a woman on the first floor.
- Where were your parents born?
- What is your first language?
- Are you disabled?
- I don't allow animals, so I can't allow your service dog.
- I don't rent to people with kids.

- Are you pregnant? I don't want a baby disturbing the other tenants.
- Where do your kids go to school?
- Do you go to the church in this neighborhood?

PERSONAL QUESTIONS TO AVOID

You should also avoid questions about marital status, sexual orientation, source of income, age, or any other possible protected class just to be on the safe side, at least if you're not very sure of the laws in your state. These types of questions can open the door to trouble:

- Are you married?
- Are you divorced?
- Are you gay?
- How old are you?
- (To a man:) I think having your boyfriend visit will make the other tenants uncomfortable.
- You're going to have to pay a higher security deposit because your income is from unemployment benefits and I'm afraid I might have to evict you in the future.

AVOID QUESTIONS OUTSIDE YOUR NORMAL QUALIFYING STANDARDS

You must have the same qualifying standards for all prospective tenants. Set a list of questions that you'll ask everyone. You can be accused of discrimination if you don't follow the exact same procedures for everyone.

For example, while it's perfectly legal to perform credit checks on tenants as long as they give their consent, you can't perform credit checks only on certain groups of people. Another example would be if you asked people who were poorly dressed about their eviction history or criminal convictions, but you ignore such questions for people who present a more acceptable appearance.

REFERENCES

Outside of prohibited questions, you're usually safe if you apply the same standards to everyone who submits a rental application. The easiest and least expensive way of doing this is to ask them to name references on the application: employer, past landlord, and one or more personal contacts.

You're entitled to call each and every reference, and you should do so. Just do it with all applications.

TENANT SCREENING SERVICES

(Source: Thebalance.com. We publish unbiased reviews; our opinions are our own and are not influenced by payments from advertisers. Learn about our independent review process and partners in our advertiser disclosure. updated February 26, 2021)

We evaluated more than a dozen tenant screening services and selected the best based on their reputation, features offered, ease of use, and customer ratings. Here are our top picks to aid in your tenant screening process.

THE 7 BEST TENANT SCREENING SERVICES OF 2021

- **Best Overall:** RentPrep
- **Runner Up, Best Overall:** MyRental
- **Best Price:** Avail
- **Best for Quick Screening:** National Tenant Network
- **Best for Additional Features:** TurboTenant
- **Best for Screening Directly from a Credit Bureau:** SmartMove
- **Best for À La Carte Services:** LeaseRunner
- **Best overall:** RentPrep

Fidelis Screening Solutions has been used by property management companies and large employers to provide background checks since it was founded in 2007. The company created RentPrep to cater to smaller landlords so they wouldn't get lost in the shuffle of big firms.

RentPrep's team of in-house, Fair Credit Reporting Act (FCRA)-certified screeners performs over 30,000 tenant screenings annually, and the city of Cedar Rapids, Iowa, made them their official tenant screening provider. The company's outstanding reputation and comprehensive offerings are why we named it best overall.

RentPrep provides criminal background checks; address history; tenant Social Security number verification; nationwide eviction data; and lien, bankruptcy, and judgment information. This data is verified by screeners to ensure accuracy and up-to-date results.

Landlords can generally get their tenant screening results within one hour during normal business hours. RentPrep also has great customer reviews. Customers like their quick turn-around time, and the thing that really makes them stand out is that they use live screeners.

Like all of our best tenant screening services, RentPrep is easy to use for both tenants and landlords, and you can contact customer support via email or by phone (Monday through Saturday).

Runner up, best overall: MyRental

MyRental is a service of CoreLogic Rental Property Solutions, a company formed in 2010 that has locations throughout the U.S. MyRental was created to serve independent landlords, real estate agents, and property managers. MyRental updates its site 24 hours a day and its databases undergo seven layers of quality control in order to verify its data.

MyRental provides criminal background checks, address history, multi-state criminal record searches, and terrorist reports, as well as some unique features including a Safe Rent Score and a Landlord Acceptance Rate. These tools can be used by landlords when deciding if a tenant is qualified or not.

MyRental is easy for landlords and tenants to use and can be accessed at any time, which is convenient if you're working after normal business hours. Landlords receive screening results, typically within an hour, to their online dashboard. However, live screeners don't verify reports. Nevertheless, customers have positive things to say about MyRental's dashboard, quick turnaround time, and efficient customer service. They also like the other metrics they're given to measure tenant qualifications outside of the usual credit history and eviction checks. The thoroughness of MyRental's screening and its constantly updated data are why we named it our runner-up.

Best price: Avail

Avail was created as a property management software platform specifically for do-it-yourself landlords. The company was founded in 2013 and is a one-stop-shop for landlords because it offers tenant screening services as well as rent collection, property marketing tools, and lease management. Avail has an A+ rating with the BBB but is not accredited.2

They specialize in offering a wide array of services to smaller landlords who own up to 10 properties but also offer packages that are appropriate for larger portfolios. The company is used by 150,000 landlords and has tons of educational material on its website about managing rental properties.

Avail is highly rated by customers who like being able to screen their tenants and manage their properties in one place. Avail is easy to use on all devices and has an app for users to download. Their pricing scale starts at free and offers limited services which include credit and criminal screening. Avail also passes all tenant application fees on to applicants.

Best for quick screening: National Tenant Network

National Tenant Network (NTN) is headquartered in Oregon and has 35 regional offices around the country, with dedicated agents to help landlords screen tenants. The company has been in business for more than 35 years, which makes them the oldest tenant screening company around. NTN has an A+ rating from the BBB but is not accredited.

NTN is a boutique service that takes a custom approach to each application. The company is ideal if you want to quickly screen an applicant and receive a recommendation to accept the tenant or not because you don't have to sift through complicated reports. Instead, NTN gives every applicant a score from zero to 100, which makes it very easy to use. This score is usually generated within minutes of submitting the application, which is why we named NTN best for quick screening.

National Tenant Network's goal is to help landlords identify whether an applicant will be a good tenant. They have positive reviews for customer service and keeping their eviction information up to date. The company offers services to landlords big and small.

Best for additional features: TurboTenant

TurboTenant was developed in 2015 and is used by over 50,000 landlords for property management, marketing, and tenant screening. It's another all-in-one platform similar to Avail that is good for landlords, real estate agents, and property managers who want the convenience of marketing vacant rental listings and screening potential tenants all on one site.

TurboTenant caters to landlords with up to 100 properties, but not necessarily those with huge portfolios. It offers the convenient option of having tenants complete a rental application right on the website, pay for the screening, and send the results to the landlord. It also has flyer templates so you can post vacant rental listings quickly across multiple websites. These extra options are why we named TurboTenant best for additional features.

TurboTenant boasts positive customer reviews, especially from customers who appreciate having multiple ways to market their listing on the site and report success finding tenants It's a user-friendly site with multiple ways to contact customer service.

TurboTenant is another à la carte tenant screening software. They don't offer tiers, packages, or monthly pricing options. Instead, it's free to sign up, free to post and market rental listings, but there are charges for screening tenants. These charges can be passed to the applicant in the form of an application fee.

Best for screening directly from a credit bureau: SmartMove

SmartMove was founded in 2008 as one of the first web-based tenant screening solutions for smaller landlords who are busy and want to be able to log on and have a decision in minutes. It screens tenants directly through TransUnion, one of the three major credit bureaus. The unique nature of screening directly through a credit bureau is why we chose to highlight the company in our review—it's in a class by itself.

SmartMove is great because it gives landlords the comfort of getting tenant insights directly from a major credit bureau while also making tenants feel secure by not passing their sensitive personal information directly to landlords. Instead, the tenant uses the site themselves, and the landlord receives a SmartMove credit score using the same scoring method that TransUnion uses. Then, like National Tenant Network, SmartMove gives the landlord a recommendation of whether or not to accept the applicant as a tenant.

SmartMove is easy to use, provides robust security protocols for applicant's information, and offers online customer support. Customers also like its affiliation with TransUnion. However, landlords aren't in control and, therefore, can't get a decision until the tenant completes the application.

Best for à la carte services: LeaseRunner

LeaseRunner was founded in 2011 and was a finalist for an Inman News Innovator Award the same year. It has an A+ rating with the Better Business Bureau but is not accredited. Landlords, real estate agents, and property managers in over 2,000 cities across the country use LeaseRunner, which doesn't offer any packages but offers a plethora of à la carte service options.

LeaseRunner is ideal for landlords who want to pick and choose individual background reports rather than purchasing a package, and the company's customers report being happy with its offerings. LeaseRunner's friendly and informative customer service agents are praised, and the site is easy to use and gives you a thorough understanding of the tenant screening process.

WHAT IS A TENANT SCREENING SERVICE?

A tenant screening service is a company that provides background data on a prospective tenant. Depending on the services you choose, this can include eviction history, credit reports, criminal background checks, and more. Screening services are typically used by landlords, real estate agents, and property managers of all sizes.

Tenant screening services help landlords know who will potentially be renting their property. They're necessary because the more the landlord knows about the tenant's eviction history, credit score, etc., the more they can predict if they will be a suitable tenant. For example, a tenant with no evictions and a high credit score is less likely to not pay rent in fear of harming their credit score.

HOW DO TENANT SCREENING SERVICES WORK?

Reputable screening services follow state and federal guidelines and information privacy acts to provide background information including eviction reports, Social Security number verifications, credit reports, and criminal history reports. This data is gathered, offered to the tenant when necessary, and is then provided in report form to the landlord or property manager.

HOW MUCH DOES THE BEST TENANT SCREENING COST?

Tenant screening services can be purchased individually or as bundles. As the landlord, you can choose which screening services are important to you and what your budget will allow. Some of the services are paid monthly and others are paid per report. Still others can be paid directly by the tenant. You can choose the screening service that suits your budget and method of payment.

You can order an individual eviction report for as little as $7.99. You can choose to have the tenants pay for their own reports—typically about $55 for credit and criminal background reports—or you can choose a package deal for as little as $5 per month per unit.

IS TENANT SCREENING WORTH THE COST?

Regardless of the size of your rental portfolio, tenant screening services are definitely worth the cost. It's far better to pay small fees upfront, rather than run the risk of thousands of dollars in eviction costs, unpaid rent, and damaged property.

Of course, tenant screening services can't guarantee that none of these will happen. However, they are less likely to happen if you rent your property to a well-qualified tenant. This is because qualified tenants are less likely to risk their credit and eviction history by not paying rent.

All landlords and property managers should generally use tenant screening services. It doesn't matter if you own one single-family home or 500 apartments. Your goal is to make the highest return on your investment. Tenant screening services help you do just that by reducing the chances of evictions, excessive property damage, and/or months of unpaid rent.

HOW WE CHOSE TENANT SCREENING SERVICES

To find the best tenant screening services, we looked at 15 different companies. We researched them to find out how reputable they are, what their customer reviews reported, their individual pricing structures, ease of use, turnaround times, and what screening services they offer. To finalize our list of the best, we chose the screening services that offer diverse services, quick turnaround times, and positive reviews.

Disclaimer: The author has not verified the information, and anyone contemplating using any of these companies should do their own research and verify costs. Additionally, there are other screening services you can find on the internet. Bottom line, having the right tenant can either make or break your business, and a tenant screening service of your choice should be used to make sure you chose the best possible tenant commensurate with the property you are trying to rent out.

Always remember the property is not the problem, the problem is caused by poor tenant selection.

WEBSITES FOR ADVERTISING YOUR RENTAL PROPERTY

- **Craigslist.com** has categories for almost everything, including properties for rent, for sale, etc. Listings are free, and you can write your own ads and include photos. The major drawback is that you will get many inquiries and scammers.
- **Zillow.com** is the leading real estate and rental marketplace dedicated to empowering consumers with data, inspiration, and knowledge. You can post a rental through Zillow Rental Manager for free.
- **Hotpads**, a leading map-based apartment and home rental search brand, is a top destination for renters in urban areas across the United States.
- **RentalHouses.com** operates as an online source of information about available houses for rent and other types of rental homes.
- **Realtor.com** gathers property info to provide the most comprehensive source of home data. The interface is a little less straightforward and attractive than sites like Zillow, but it provides a simple search function for price and location.
- **Padmapper.com** has a fun, interactive map that allows prospective renters to set a price, choose the number of bedrooms, and look at properties in cities across North America that suit that price range. Renters will not see your actual listing during the initial search but will be able to view it when they dig a little deeper.
- **Lovely.com** allows prospective tenants to search and connect with rental owners. It has a straightforward, graphic format with an interactive map. The latest listings show up in red on the map so renters can see what is fresh on the market. It is also easy for tenants to see whether a property is pet-friendly, and there is a list of amenities you will need to fill out.

- **Rentals.com** is an online source for houses, apartments, condos, and townhouses for rent. It is easy for prospective tenants to search for precisely the type of home they want, with searches compiled into condos, lofts, duplexes, and more. Less information is required about amenities, and your contact information and availability are flagged to encourage people to call.

- **Rentdigs.com** lists all types of rental properties and pet-friendly apartments and features free photo listings. Prospective tenants can get information on rentals as well as rent-to-own homes and obtain moving company quotes.

- **Rent.com** allows users to search for apartments, houses, and townhouses. It is one of the higher-traffic sites on the list, so it is worth looking into when you are ready to connect with potential tenants.

- **Zumper.com** lists hundreds of thousands of homes and apartments for rent and allows users to filter your their results by price, bedrooms, neighborhood, pets. It is a value-added site that offers neighborhood information and city guides for your tenants. Its initial listings feature minimal information and a single photo, but its detailed listings offer you the opportunity to add an engaging paragraph about your property.

- **Airbnb.com** is a home rental site that connects a community of homeowners directly to customers seeking short-term rentals. Airbnb is a dominant player in the home rental sharing economy or peer-to-peer (P2P) activity of providing or sharing access to goods and services.

- **Apartments.com** and **Apartmentfinder.com** provide free information on long-term rentals of apartments and condos. These sites offer deals and can provide upfront savings to users who end up renting through the site.

- **VRBO.com** (Vacation Rentals by Owners) is a top-ranked site specializing in vacation rental homes, apartments, condos, B&B cabins, beach houses, villas, and so on.
- **Nextdoor.com** has carved out a unique space on the Internet as a private social networking site for local neighborhoods, with 80% of neighborhoods across the US relying on information and services shared by members. It is a popular site for Realtors to brand their services and for landlords to list rentals to a highly engaged and active local community.
- **Facebook.com** offers discussion groups on many topics, including rentals. It is a great way to get the word out to your Facebook contacts about a rental property.
- **HomeAway.com** has been around longer than Airbnb and is similar in that it guides registered users to its inventory of short-term rentals. Unlike Airbnb, however, HomeAway.com offers rentals of entire properties instead of rooms, hostels, or even beds. As such, this site is more popular with property managers and individual owners. HomeAway owns VRBO and uses that site to cater to short-term vacation rentals looking for single rooms or partial accommodations along the lines of Airbnb.
- **Walk Score.com** is a niche site whose stated mission is to promote walkable neighborhoods for those residing in apartments. It appeals to renters concerned with transportation costs, commute times, access to public transportation, or a property's proximity to activities, businesses, schools, and so on.
- **Sublet.com** is not just about sublets. Every type of rental can be listed here: short term, long-term, vacation, furnished or unfurnished, and room rentals. Landlords can post a Standard listing for free or purchase a Premium listing that can receive up to 500 times more

leads. Tenant screening, employment, and criminal background investigation services are provided for a fee based on the market you are listing in.

- The move.com is a one-stop shop that provides services for experienced renters or buyers who know exactly where they want to live and what they are looking for in a home or apartment. It also caters to seniors who may require assisted living, continuing care, or independent living facilities. This company has listings that are viewed by a customer base of 40 million people. It also provides many helpful tips and links on topics such as finding pet-friendly rentals, deciding whether to rent or buy, and tips for painting, decorating, and moving.

- People with Pets.com appeals to renters who own pets (72% of tenants in the United States). The site is a national directory of pet-friendly homes, apartments, and hotels. Renters can use the site at no charge; property owners and managers pay for advertising their pet-friendly properties.

MAKE-READY CHECKLIST FOR RENTAL PROPERTY

Task	Date finished	Initials
1.Make sure stove, refrigerator, and dishwasher are clean.	_____	_____
2.Make sure kitchen cabinets are clean and cabinet doors open and close properly.	_____	_____
3.Clean and caulk tub/shower, clean medicine cabinet, clean and secure toilet and seat.	_____	_____
4.Make sure all windows open and close, have locks, and are clean.	_____	_____
5.Replace broken window blinds and ensure that blinds work properly.	_____	_____
6.Check furnace filter and change if necessary.	_____	_____
7.Make sure garage is clean.	_____	_____
8.Make sure all doors open and close properly and storm doors have closers and chains.	_____	_____
9.Make sure there are no broken screens or broken glass on storm windows and doors.	_____	_____
10.Mow yard and remove junk.	_____	_____
11.Make sure all electrical outlets work.	_____	_____
12.Replace all burned-out light bulbs.	_____	_____
13.Make sure smoke and carbon monoxide detectors are working properly.	_____	_____
14.Make sure there is one carbon monoxide detector on each finished floor.	_____	_____
15.Make sure there is one smoke detector in each bedroom, one in basement, and one between living room and kitchen.	_____	_____
16.Check all closets to make sure they are clean and have closet poles.	_____	_____
17.Check all ceiling fans to make sure they work and are clean.	_____	_____

18. Make sure there are no leaks under kitchen and bathroom sinks and faucets work properly. _____   _____

19. Check/wipe all walls to make sure they are clean; touch up with paint as necessary. _____   _____

20. Check for mold in basement and under kitchen and bathroom sinks and clean with mold spray as needed. _____   _____

21. Make sure entire house has been cleaned. _____   _____

22. Make sure gutters are clean. _____   _____

23. Replace any missing corners on siding. _____   _____

24. Make sure all drains work properly. _____   _____

25. Make sure all interior and exterior handrails are secured. _____   _____

26. Make sure carpet is clean. _____   _____

Notes:

_____

Date completed_____

Signature_____

REHAB WORKSHEET BLANK

Rehab Worksheet (Blank)								
Address								
1.PURCHASE COSTS					Good	Better	Best	
Loan Origination			PURCHASE PRICE					
Appraisal			PURCHASE COSTS		$ -	$ -	$ -	
Credit Report			HOLDING COSTS		$ -	$ -	$ -	
Title Insurance			RENOVATION COSTS		$ -	$ -	$ -	
Escrow Fee								
Recording Fee					$ -	$ -	$ -	
Other								
TOTAL PURCHASE COSTS	$ -							
			PROPOSED SALES PRICE					
			Commission					
2.HOLDING COSTS			Title Insurance					
Interest			Document Stamps					
Property Taxes			Other					
Insurance			Other					
Utilities			Other					
Gas, Water, Sewer, Electrical								
Trash service			Net Proceeds To Seller		$ -	$ -	$ -	
Other								
TOTAL HOLDING COSTS	$ -		Total Profit / Loss		$ -	$ -	$ -	
3.RENOVATION COSTS			NOTES:					
Clean up/Demolition								
Electrical								
Plumbing								
Painting/drywall								
Kitchen Remodel								
Bathroom Remodel								
Flooring								
Carpet								
Roof, Siding, Windows								
Landscape/Lawn								
Other								
SUBTOTAL RENOVATION COST	$ -							
TOTAL COSTS[1,2,3]	$ -							
(Only change highlighted areas)								

REHAB WORKSHEET SAMPLE

Rehab Worksheet (Sample)

Address				Good	Better	Best
1.PURCHASE COSTS				Good	Better	Best
Loan Origination	$ 1,000.00		PURCHASE PRICE	$80,000.00	$75,000.00	$70,000.00
Appraisal	$ 400.00		PURCHASE COSTS	$ 2,120.00	$ 2,120.00	$ 2,120.00
Credit Report	$ 70.00		HOLDING COSTS	$ 4,700.00	$ 4,700.00	$ 4,700.00
Title Insurance	$ 425.00		RENOVATION COSTS	$ 26,000.00	$ 26,000.00	$ 26,000.00
Escrow Fee	$ 175.00					
Recording Fee	$ 50.00			$112,820.00	$107,820.00	$102,820.00
Other						
TOTAL PURCHASE COSTS	$ 2,120.00					
			PROPOSED SALES PRICE	$120,000.00	$130,000.00	$135,000.00
			Commission	$ 7,200.00	$ 7,800.00	$ 8,100.00
2.HOLDING COSTS			Title Insurance	$ 200.00	$ 210.00	$ 213.00
Interest	$ 3,600.00		Document Stamps	$ 270.00	$ 292.50	$ 303.75
Property Taxes	$ 600.00		Other			
Insurance	$ 150.00		Other			
Utilities			Other			
Gas, Water, Sewer, Electrical	$ 350.00					
Trash service			Net Proceeds To Seller	$112,330.00	$121,697.50	$126,383.25
Other						
TOTAL HOLDING COSTS	$ 4,700.00		Total Profit / Loss	$ (490.00)	$ 13,877.50	$ 23,563.25
3.RENOVATION COSTS			NOTES:			
Clean up/Demolition	$ 1,000.00					
Electrical	$ 500.00					
Plumbing	$ 500.00					
labor	$ 11,000.00					
materials	$ 10,000.00					
Carpet	$ 2,500.00					
Roof, Siding, Windows						
Landscape/Lawn	$ 500.00					
Other						
SUBTOTAL RENOVATION COS	$ 26,000.00					
TOTAL COSTS[1,2,3]	$ 32,820.00					
(Only change highlighted areas)						

REMODELING WORKSHEET

Property Address _____ Date _____

Remodeling to be completed   Cost   Sub Total

Kitchen	Item	Cost	Sub Total
1	_____	_____	
2	_____	_____	
3	_____	_____	
4	_____	_____	
5	_____	_____	
6	_____	_____	
7	_____	_____	
8	_____	_____	

Bathroom	Item	Cost	Sub Total
1	_____	_____	
2	_____	_____	
3	_____	_____	
4	_____	_____	
5	_____	_____	

Living Room	Item	Cost	Sub Total
1			
2			
3			
4			
5			

Dining Room	Item	Cost	Sub Total
1			
2			
3			

Bedroom 1	Item	Cost	Sub Total
1			
2			
3			
4			

Bedroom 2	Item	Cost	Sub Total
1			
2			
3			
4			

Bedroom 3	Item	Cost	Sub Total
1			
2			
3			
4			

Basement	Item	Cost	Sub Total
1			
2			
3			
4			

Exterior	Item	Cost	Sub Total
1			
2			
3			
4			
5			

Misc	Item	Cost	Sub Total
1	_____	_____
2	_____	_____
3	_____	_____
4	_____	_____
5	_____	_____

PROPERTY CHECKLIST

Print out a few copies of this checklist to use as you visit prospective properties.

Having information on each property can help you to compare properties and will make your final decision much easier.

Date _____

Address _____ Price _____

Property taxes _____

How long has it been on the market? _____

Foreclosure _____ yes _____ no Other _____

Age of property _____ Neighborhood/Subdivision _____

Corner lot __ yes __ no

Overall impression of Area/Neighborhood __ Acceptable __ Not acceptable

Overall impression of properties on either side and /across from subject property __ Acceptable __ Not acceptable __ Other _____

Style

__ 2.5 Story __ 2 Story __ Bungalow __ Multi level __ Ranch __ Split entry

__ Raised ranch __ Tri-level __ Cape Cod __ Townhouse __ Condo __ Other

_____

Type of Construction

__ Wood __ Brick __ Stone __ Stucco __ Vinyl siding __ Aluminum siding __ ther

_____

Exterior Features

Roof type _____

Roof condition ____ Good ____ Fair ____ Acceptable __ Needs replaced

Fenced ____ yes ____ no Porch ____ yes ____ no Deck __ yes ____ no

Patio __yes __no   Deck __yes ___no

Other_____

_____

Paint ___ Acceptable ___ Needs painted

Other_____

_____

Garage

___ 1 car __ 2 cars __Attached __Detached __ Carport

___ no garage __off-street parking

Central AC __ yes __no   Window units __yes __no # of units _____

Interior Features

Kitchen

Eat-In __yes__no_____Size _____

Type of flooring __Ceramic tile __Wood floors__ Linoleum __   Other _____

Appliances __ yes __no   Stove__yes __ no

Refrigerator __yes __ no   Dishwasher __yes __ no   Other _____

Condition of cabinets __ new__old   Painted: __yes __no

Needs replacing __yes __no

Dining Room

__yes __no Size _____   Carpet yes__no__ Wood floors yes__no__

Living Room

Size _____ Carpet __yes __no   Wood floors yes __no__

Other_____

Den/Family room Size _____

Carpet __yes __no   Wood floors yes __ no__

Other rooms_____

Total bedrooms_____

Bedroom 1 size _____ Carpet __yes __no Wood floors yes __ no

Other _____

Bedroom 2 size _____ Carpet __yes __no Wood floors yes __ no

Other _____

Bedroom 3 size _____ Carpet __yes __no Wood floors yes __ no

Other _____

Bedroom 4 size _____ Carpet __yes __no Wood floors yes __ no

Other _____

_____

Total bathrooms _____

_____ Full_____ 3/4_____ 1/2_____ 1/4

Master bath ___ yes ___ no Flooring type_____

Guest/powder bath ___ yes ___ no Flooring type_____

Other_____

_____

Laundry room

Location _____ Washer ___yes ___no Dryer ___yes ___no

Other_____

_____

Basement ___yes ___no Finished ___yes ___no _____

Flooring Carpet _____Tile _____ Other _____

Utilities

Type of Heating

_____Gas_____Steam ___Hot water _____Electric _____ Oil

Age of System _____

Age/Capacity of water heater_____ Gas_____ Electric_____

Electrical service

_____Fuses _____Circuit breakers

Plumbing

___Galvanized ___Copper ___Other _____

Sump pump/Drainage system: ___yes ___no

Sewer connected to public sewer ___yes ___no   Septic ____yes ____no
Other_____

Proximity to:

_____Schools _____Shopping _____Highways _____Religious   institutions
_____Downtown _____ Hospitals Other

_____

_____

Other things of interest nearby:

_____

_____

Recent sales of comparable properties in neighborhood

Address _____   Sq. Ft _____

Price _____

# of bedrooms _____ # of baths____

Other features_____

_____

Address _____   Sq. Ft _____

Price _____

# of bedrooms _____ # of baths_____

Other features_____

_____

Address _____   Sq. Ft _____

Price _____

# of bedrooms _____ # of baths_____

Other features_____

_____

Notes

_____

_____

_____

_____

_____

_____

_____

_____

_____

_____

_____

STATEMENT OF ASSETS AND LIABILITIES

Financial Statement

Name_____Email_____ Telephone_____

Asset/Investment	Current value	Ownership Individual=I, Joint =J
1. Checking acct. bal.	$_____	_____
2. Savings acct. bal.	$_____	_____
3. Certificate of deposit	$_____	_____
4. Stocks	$_____	_____
5.Mutual funds	$_____	_____
6.Other securities	$_____	_____
7.Your retirement (401K,Ira's)	$_____	_____
8. Your spouse's retirement if applicable	$_____	_____
9. Business /partnerships if applicable	$_____	_____
10.Cash value life insurance	$_____	_____
11. Face value of life insurance	$_____	_____
12. Real estate(personal residence)	$_____	_____
13. Real estate portfolio(please explain)	$_____	_____
14. Other assets(please explain)	$_____	

For # 13 and # 14 explain
on separate sheet

Total Assets $_____

Debt

	Current value	Ownership
1.Credit cards etc	$_____	_____
2.Real estate personal residence	$_____	_____
3. Real estate portfolio	$_____	_____
4.Car loans if applicable)	$_____	_____
5.Other debt (Please describe)	$_____	_____

 # 5 explain on separate sheet

Total debt $_____

Assets - liabilities= Net worth $_____

Date   _____

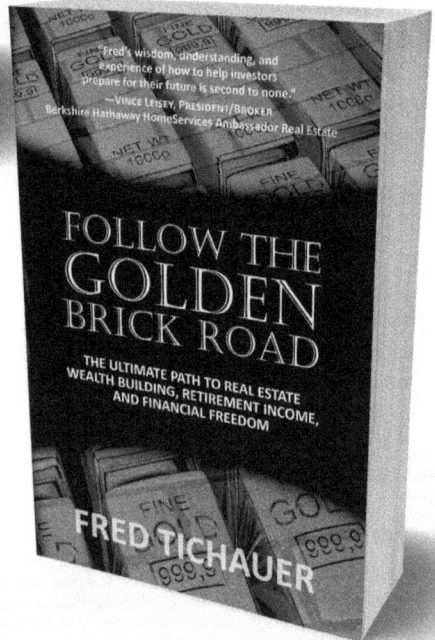

www.ingramcontent.com/pod-product-compliance
Lightning Source LLC
Chambersburg PA
CBHW021924190326
41519CB00009B/899